DATE DUE

APR 2 3 2015			

Women Leaders Who Changed the World

Heather Ball

rosen publishing's
**rosen
central**

To J.W.C.

This edition first published in 2012 by:

The Rosen Publishing Group, Inc.
29 East 21st Street
New York, NY 10010

Additional end matter and content copyright © 2012 by The Rosen Publishing Group, Inc. With additional material by Susan Meyer.

All rights reserved. No part of this publication may be reproduced, stored in a retrieval system or transmitted, in any form or by any means, without the prior written consent of the publisher.

Library of Congress Cataloging-in-Publication Data

Ball, Heather, 1978–
Women leaders who changed the world/Heather Ball.
    p. cm.—(Great women of achievement)
Rev. ed. of: Great women leaders. Toronto, Ontario: Second Story Press, 2004.
Includes bibliographical references and index.
ISBN 978-1-4488-6000-5 (library binding)
1. Women—Biography—Juvenile literature. 2. Leadership in women—Juvenile literature. I. Ball, Heather, 1978– Great women leaders. II. Title.
HQ1123.B354 2012
920.72—dc23
[B]

2011033321

2012 #24 95

Manufactured in the United States of America

CPSIA Compliance Information: Batch #W12YA: For further information, contact Rosen Publishing, New York, New York, at 1-800-237-9932.

First published by Second Story Press, Canada 2004, Copyright © Heather Ball, 2004.

Frances Rooney, Editor

Contents

Introduction

Why write a book about women leaders? Why not write about leaders in general, whether they're men or women? I remember when I was in school, history was one of my favorite subjects. I loved hearing about brave men who led others toward a better world, who dared to do things differently and introduced new ways of thinking. But something has always bothered me. It all seemed uneven. I couldn't help but ask myself one question: Where are all the women?

The deeds of women have not always been acknowledged. Maybe it's because, traditionally, most societies have been *patriarchal*, meaning "run by men." Until the twentieth century, women didn't have many choices for what they could do with their lives. Women could not vote in elections, most could not own property or go to college. Women make up half of the world's population and even today are not involved in a lot of decision-making. It's hard to believe that the United States, one of the most developed nations, has never elected a woman as leader. In fact, only about fourteen countries have had a woman president or prime minister. Only 14 percent of members of Parliament worldwide are women.

Despite these statistics, it's important to know that there are many women who show leadership every day and accomplish great things. In this book, you will read about some incredible woman leaders. Some names you may have heard before. Others you will know for the first time. They come from Africa, Southeast Asia, the Middle East, and North America. They maintain different religious and spiritual beliefs. They have completed varying levels of education. They have worked for the environment, for peace, and for civil rights. Their stories take place throughout history, from thousands of years ago right up to today. Despite being so different from one another, these women have many things in common.

Past or present, all of the women in this book used their intelligence to solve problems. They were never afraid to question the world around them, to challenge what they thought was wrong. All faced prejudice in one form or another. They were looked down upon because of skin color, religion, or for the simple fact of being female. They were teased, called names, and even threatened, but they were strong and determined and never gave up. Most important, they believed in themselves and their ability to make a difference.

Many of these women had no idea that they would become great leaders. Hatshepsut thought she would be a pharaoh's wife, not a pharaoh. Golda Meir wanted to spend her life on a communal farm. Aung San Suu Kyi saw herself as a scholar, not a politician. Often, their accomplishments came about from simple, but important actions. Rosa Parks did not give up her seat on a bus. Wangari Maathai grew trees in her backyard.

If you have ever thought to yourself, "I can't do it; one person can't make a difference," then I hope you will be inspired by these stories. Whether you want to start a club for others who share your interests, run for class president, or get people together to fight for a cause that you truly believe in—you *can* do it! There is still a long way to go in the area of gender equality, but progress is being made every day. These women are proof of that. All of them show that women can do great things and make the world a better place for everyone.

Chapter 1

Hatshepsut

Circa 1505–1455 BCE

It is over thirty-five hundred years ago in mysterious ancient Egypt, home of columned temples, the pyramids and the lavish tombs of royalty. The pharaoh, the country's king, who was believed to be part human, part god, surveys the great land and ponders the enormous responsibilities. Some of these include planning military strategies, proclaiming laws, and most important, preserving *maat*, the Egyptian idea of universal order and balance.

Life in ancient Egypt was very different from what we know today. People did not have the choices we now enjoy. Men mainly worked in the fields or did other kinds of demanding outdoor physical labor. Some worked as merchants or craftsmen. If they were lucky enough to be able to read and write, they could work as a scribe and write letters for the pharaoh or document events in hieroglyphs, Egypt's written language of pictures. Women's choices were even more limited, and their main occupation was running their household, although some worked as midwives, maids for richer families, or dancers at special events. Houses were built of bricks made from a mixture of mud, straw, and pebbles, and of course had no electricity or running water. Temperatures, then as now, often reached over 104 degrees Fahrenheit (40 degrees Celsius), and because of the incredible heat, both men and women shaved their heads to keep cool and wore wigs out in public. Staying bald actually served a second purpose, which was to protect against lice and disease. Although Egyptians loved to decorate themselves, the basics of fashion were practical. They wore simple sandals made from reeds and clothing made from linen, a light fabric woven from flaxseed plants that lets air pass through easily and does not absorb the heat of the sun. To protect their eyes from the sun's

This fresco was painted on the wall in Hatshepsut's temple in Egypt. Many of the frescoes are believed to be autobiographical depictions of events from Hatshepsut's life.

harsh glare, women and men painted around their eyelids with kohl, a dark black eyeliner.

Hatshepsut's father was Tuthmosis I, who had no royal blood himself but was chosen to become pharaoh because he was an accomplished warrior who led the country in many military victories. Her mother, Queen Ahmose, possessed great wisdom and as "God's Wife," the title given to the queen of Egypt, had a lot of influence.

It is believed that Hatshepsut was her father's favorite child, and she grew up with every opportunity and advantage. She had private tutors who probably taught her to read and write. Because she was the king's only daughter, some stories say she might have even participated in activities reserved for boys, such as crocodile hunting—certainly not your everyday after-school activity! The best part of her childhood was traveling across the country with her father, which allowed her to gain an appreciation for the wonders of the land at a young age. Seeing the Nile River, the pyramids, temples, and monuments, she felt a deep admiration for what Tuthmosis I and other pharaohs before him had accomplished.

Princess Hatshepsut might have been as young as twelve years old when she got married after the death of her father. Because she was the only true royal daughter, she married the successor to the throne and was crowned queen of Egypt. As queen, she was responsible for running the palace and acted as a valuable advisor to the pharaoh. It was also her responsibility to produce an heir to the throne, ensuring that the royal bloodlines were not broken. By today's standards Hatshepsut was quite restricted. But based on ancient letters and court documents, it seems that many women of ancient Egypt enjoyed greater freedom than other women of the time. Legally, they were allowed to own, sell, and inherit land and possessions, even fight for their rights in court. While other ancient societies, such as Greece and Rome, frowned upon a woman stepping outside the home unescorted, Egyptian women walked freely to the market and were not required to live with a man if their husbands died or if they never married.

Some have called Hatshepsut history's first great woman. The biography of a court official named Ineni, who had served three earlier pharaohs, claimed that "Egypt was made to labor with bowed head for her ... the mistress of command, whose plans are excellent."

Hatshepsut's husband, Tuthmosis II, was never very healthy and died after only a few years as king. Since the couple had no children, all of Egypt wondered who would be named the next ruler. The only possible heir (traditionally, the pharaoh was male) was Hatshepsut's stepson, the young Tuthmosis III. But with the new heir came a new problem; he was only a small child who had no idea how to reign over a mighty kingdom. Hatshepsut was therefore appointed as his regent, the person who would take over his duties and act as his representative until he grew up.

Hatshepsut quickly got used to taking a more dominant role in the ruling of her country. She sent armies to Nubia and Palestine to protect Egypt's borders, made decisions on how to divide the country's taxes, led government meetings, and made sure the members of the powerful and wealthy priesthood were satisfied with her work. Egypt was flourishing as a nation, and it became obvious that not only was Hatshepsut good at ruling, she also enjoyed it. Officially, she showed herself in public standing behind Tuthmosis III, as she was still considered his regent. Eventually, however, she began standing next to him, and soon in front. After about seven years of serving as leader in practice but without the title, she felt she deserved recognition for her hard work and experience. In one of the boldest moves Egypt had ever seen, and in an act of amazing self-confidence, Hatshepsut declared herself pharaoh, the top male position in the country.

Appearance was important in ancient Egypt, especially for royalty. The traditional clothing of the pharaoh was a kilt (*shendyt*), a headdress (*nemes*), a snake-like symbol above the forehead of a king's crown (*uraeus*), and a long beard made of gold. Hatshepsut wore the full outfit at public assemblies, causing some to believe she wished to be seen as a male ruler. Since traditional costume for a female ruler did not exist at the time, it is more likely that she was

This white limestone statue is called "Seated Figure of Hatshepsut." Hatshepsut strongly believed in restoring the beauty of Egypt during her reign.

the pharaoh and would therefore dress the part, no matter what her gender.

Hatshepsut ruled very differently from her father. Instead of sending out armies to conquer neighboring nations, she was more concerned with restoring the beauty of her own. Remembering the pride she had felt as a child touring the country, she built many beautiful statues and repaired temples crumbling from age and weather. She also left her mark by having two obelisks built, tall stone monuments with pointed tops that stand about 100 feet (30.5 m) tall. These obelisks paid tribute to Ra, the sun god, and took seven months to construct. The people of Egypt saw her accomplishments as a sign of her devotion to them and their history. It also made them proud to live in such a majestic land.

Besides her contribution to architecture, Hatshepsut cleverly gained the people's favor in other ways. She made it clear that her father had been grooming her for the position of pharaoh since she was young, although this was probably not the case. She also spread a tale about her conception, which is depicted on the walls of her mortuary tomb, Deir el-Bahri. It tells of how her mother was visited by the god Amen-Re disguised as Tuthmosis I. The tale says that Ahmose became pregnant with Hatshepsut by a life-giving breath from the god's divine lungs. The story was meant to leave no doubt in the people's minds that she had godly blood in her veins, just like all male rulers.

> In addition to many riches, Hatshepsut's ships brought back people from Punt, and animals such as baboons, monkeys, dogs, and a leopard. These were brought through the streets of Thebes on their way to the palace, to the great excitement of the Egyptian people, who were very curious about foreign lands.

Another of Hatshepsut's feats was a trade expedition of five ships sent to Punt, known today as Somalia. They returned with riches, such as myrrh trees, gold, perfume, and ivory, proving that just as much could be gained through commerce as through conquest.

Hatshepsut died around the age of fifty, but there is great controversy surrounding her death. Attempts were made to erase her from history. As the Egyptians held strong religious beliefs about death, feeling it was another stage of life, this was a supreme insult, especially to a pharaoh. Her name was chiseled off monuments and sometimes replaced with the name of Tuthmosis III. Statues of her had parts of their faces chipped off, and her name was removed from all the lists of kings so that they showed only the names of the male pharaohs. Even her mortuary temple at Deir el-Bahri was broken into and many of the scenes smashed off the walls. But who would do such a thing and why?

Some say that the architectural elegance and harmony of the Temple of Hatshepsut is only comparable with that of the Parthenon.

Nobody knows for sure. It may have been that Tuthmosis III was angry with Hatshepsut for failing to step down once he reached the age to rule, and he wanted her permanently wiped out of the country's memory. Or it may be that he respected her for the help and guidance she provided but wished to put an end to the notion that a woman could be pharaoh. The most dramatic story is that he had her murdered. But this is not really believed because she ruled long and successfully without Tuthmosis III ever expressing any desire for her to give up the throne.

Despite the attempts to erase Hatshepsut from history, many artifacts from her reign survived, allowing archeologists to piece her story together. Reassembling statues that were broken into bits as small as pebbles, they were also able to read some of the scenes drawn in hieroglyphics on the walls at Deir el-Bahri.

Hatshepsut's rule is known as a fifteen- to twenty-year time of peace and prosperity for Egypt. Although attempts were made to hide her name and accomplishments, her story has survived, an example from thousands of years ago of a woman who reigned successfully.

Chapter 2
Elizabeth Cady Stanton
1815–1902

When Elizabeth Cady was eleven, her only brother died. On the day of the funeral, Elizabeth saw her father sitting by the coffin with his head down, tears falling on the carpet. She went to him, climbed onto his lap, and gave him a bear hug. She told him she and her four sisters would always be there for him. Her father sighed and said, "I wish you were a boy."

This made no sense to Elizabeth. She did not want to be a boy. But the words did make her realize something. Even if she was not a boy, there was no reason she could not do all the things that boys did. She would grow up to be every bit as smart, brave, and accomplished as any boy.

Elizabeth was born on November 12, 1815, in Johnstown, New York. Her father, Daniel, was a judge, and her mother, Margaret, took care of their children, which was a tough job. Elizabeth had so much energy. She loved to ride and train horses. On horseback, she could jump a fence that was taller than she was. She was impossible to catch in a game of tag and was the best chess player in the neighborhood.

When Elizabeth's body wasn't running and jumping, her mind was. She would sit quietly in her father's office and listen to people who came in for legal advice. She learned a lot about not only the law, but also about how unfairly women were treated. Once married, a woman belonged to her husband and could not own anything for herself. She could not have a position in public office or vote in elections. If her husband abused her, she was not allowed to leave him. It seemed that every time Elizabeth asked her father if a woman was allowed to do something, the answer was always "no."

At Johnstown Academy, Elizabeth was the only girl in the advanced classes for math and language, and won prizes for her high grades. She also took Greek lessons taught by her neighbor. Elizabeth intended to go to college, but could not because she was a girl. So she went to an all-girl school called Emma Willard's Troy Female Seminary.

At her cousin Libby Smith's house, Elizabeth finally met other people who did not believe society's laws were fair. People discussed what could be done to change things. Elizabeth, feeling as if her mind was awakened from a long sleep, happily learned and participated in the conversations. It was during these visits that she met Henry Stanton. He was an abolitionist and gave many speeches against slavery. Henry and Elizabeth married in 1840. But Elizabeth made certain right from the start that as a wife, she would not be Henry's property. She had the word "obey" removed from the wedding ceremony and throughout her life always used both her maiden and married names.

That same year, Henry and Elizabeth sailed across the ocean to the World Anti-Slavery Convention in London, England. Lucretia Mott, a Quaker abolitionist, also attended. Although she was twenty years older than Elizabeth, the women became great friends and spent hours talking about outlawing slavery and about women's rights. They were eager to participate in the convention, but on the first day they were told that women could not sit with the men and were not allowed to talk. They had to pretend to be invisible. Elizabeth was furious. Even though some of the men were angry, too, the rules were not changed.

> **Abolitionists** believed that slavery was wrong and pushed to abolish, or completely do away with, the practice. They faced great resistance, particularly in the southern United States. Abolition was one of the conflicts over which the Civil War was fought.

When Elizabeth and Lucretia said good-bye, they knew it would not be for long. They hoped to work together on women's issues. Elizabeth and her husband returned to the United States and settled in Seneca Falls, New York. Over the next few years, Elizabeth had her first three children, all boys. It took most of Elizabeth's energy to clean the house, cook meals, and keep the children busy every day while Henry went on lecture tours. She was lonely and isolated from her friends, and later wrote that she felt like a caged lion.

In 1848, Elizabeth was thrilled to visit her friend Lucretia. There were other women there as well, women who also had heard the word "no" all their lives and were sick of

Elizabeth Cady Stanton had seven children, including the baby shown here. Harriot, who grew up to also be an activist and advocate for women.

it. They talked about how women were just as good as men, even if men had all the power. Lucretia and Elizabeth told the story of the Anti-Slavery Convention. This gave them an idea. They decided to have their own convention where men and women could sit together and women would be allowed to speak.

For the convention, Elizabeth wrote a paper called the "Declaration of Rights and Sentiments." She had never spoken to a crowd before, but despite her nervousness, she pretended she was not afraid and read her paper aloud. Some thought the ideas were crazy, especially her idea about women having the right to vote.

The new feminist ideas were discussed everywhere, and most people thought they were wrong. Women belonged at home. They had to be wives and mothers, people said. Even though she had small children to care for, Elizabeth managed to write speeches and letters to newspapers about why women deserved equal treatment.

Elizabeth met Susan B. Anthony in 1851. They liked each other right away, and Susan became Elizabeth's best friend and supporter. They were both activists interested in the same thing, women's rights.

From that first meeting, the two women shared not only a friendship but also a partnership. When one needed help, the other was always there. Each did excellent work on her own, but together they were even better. Each had her own special talents. Elizabeth's strength was writing, and Susan was a lively speaker. Together they decided what they wanted to express, Elizabeth wrote it down, and Susan shared it with the world. Even their different lifestyles contributed to the partnership. Susan never married or had children, so she could travel to conventions and meetings. One of Elizabeth's biggest challenges was how to balance work and motherhood. Her seventh and last baby was born in 1859, and Elizabeth was often exhausted. When it was hard for her to write, Susan babysat.

The women's rights movement was getting stronger, and Elizabeth found herself becoming more and more

The Wesleyan Chapel is an important historical landmark because the 1848 Seneca Falls Woman's Rights Convention assembled there. The building is currently undergoing renovation.

Bloomers came to be named for Amelia Bloomer, the publisher of the first feminist magazine in North America, *The Lily*. She was an enthusiastic promoter of the new style.

involved. She was not afraid of those who thought she was strange or crazy for wanting change. In addition to women's right to vote, she fought the dress code for women. Women had to wear many layers of long, heavy skirts that made them trip and that were often caked with dirt, mud, or snow. They also wore corsets, tight garments that made the waist look small. Corsets were so tight, they made it hard to breathe. They sometimes broke women's ribs, and, if a rib punctured a lung, it caused death. In 1851, some rebellious women, including Elizabeth, started wearing an outfit with loose, puffy shorts called bloomers. It was much more comfortable, but tradition made it scandalous for a woman to show her legs. Elizabeth walked around in her bloomers for two years.

For Elizabeth and Susan, the two most important issues were women's suffrage and changing a law known as the Women's Property Act. In 1854, Elizabeth became the first woman ever to speak in front of the legislature of New York State about these two problems. She had to write the best speech of her life and spent many sleepless nights

In the above context, **suffrage** is the right to vote in public elections. A **suffragist** is someone who supports the extension of this right, in this case to women. Women who supported women's suffrage became known as "suffragettes."

In 1872, before women were allowed to vote, Susan B. Anthony and fourteen other women in Rochester, New York, cast ballots in an election. They were arrested, and all except Susan paid the $500 bail. Susan refused and was tried by an all-male jury, who fined her $100.

working on it to get the words just right. When the day came, she stood up in front of the all-male senate and presented her case. No laws were changed, but it was a step forward. In 1860, she spoke once again in front of the senate, and this time, they listened. Married women gained the right to do business, sign contracts, and have their own money and custody of their children, all without their husband's permission.

Susan B. Anthony and Elizabeth Cady Stanton, shown here seated together, were the two great leaders of the American women's suffrage movement and fought hard for equal rights.

When the Civil War broke out in the United States in 1861, the women's movement became linked with the anti-slavery movement. With the announcement of the Emancipation Proclamation and the Thirteenth Amendment (laws freeing slaves), Elizabeth and Susan hoped women's freedom would not be far behind. But black men got the vote before women, and Elizabeth's frustration grew. The suffragists divided into two groups. Susan and Elizabeth founded the National Woman Suffrage Association (NWSA), which did not allow men as members and was seen as radical. (The other group, the American Woman Suffrage Association, had male members and conservative views.) Elizabeth was president of the NWSA for twenty-one years.

Elizabeth began a speaking tour, and, along with suffrage, lectured on topics such as education, religion, and divorce for women. She and Susan started a feminist newspaper called *The Revolution*. Elizabeth wrote, and Susan managed the finances.

Tired of the road but not tired of fighting, Elizabeth began a new project in the 1880s. She knew she and her colleagues were making history by challenging the U.S. Constitution, and it was time to tell the story. Susan and Elizabeth wrote *A History of Woman Suffrage* to record their work so far.

In 1890, the two women's organizations merged into one—the National American Woman Suffrage Association. They put their differences aside and hoped for strength in numbers. Elizabeth was elected president and Susan was vice-president. At age seventy-five, Elizabeth was even fierier than when she was a younger woman. "I get more radical as I get older," she said. When she retired two years later, she did not leave quietly. Her speech, "The Solitude of Self," is still famous today. In it, she spoke about how each person is a unique soul and must be given the rights and freedoms to be strong and independent.

Elizabeth spent the 1890s writing articles and letters that were published across the country. She also wrote *The Woman's Bible*, which challenged the way women were represented in the Bible. It angered many people and was a bestseller.

Elizabeth lived to be eighty-seven years old. She would have been proud to know that her daughter, Harriot Stanton Blatch, followed in her footsteps and campaigned for women's suffrage. The Nineteenth Amendment, which gave women the right to vote, was passed on August 26, 1920. Although she did not live to see this day, Elizabeth always fought for things that went beyond herself. She worked for future generations of daughters and granddaughters. If, at the end of her life, someone had asked Elizabeth if she was still glad she was not born a boy, you can be sure she would have said, "Yes."

Chapter 3
Mary Ann Shadd Cary

1823–1893

Harriet and Abraham Shadd, who were "free blacks," lived in Wilmington in the "slave state" of Delaware. Mary, the oldest of their thirteen children, was born on October 9, 1823. Although the lives of free blacks were far from safe or easy—most lived in poverty, and they sometimes were kidnapped and sold into slavery—Mary grew up knowing that she had a lot of potential and spent her life ignoring the customs that limited black people and women.

When she was very little, Mary noticed that her father's shoemaking shop was always full of people coming and going. With such a large family, Harriet had many mouths to feed, but Mary always helped her mother cook extra food. She soon understood that these people were not just visitors but slaves in search of freedom, running away from cruel masters.

Abraham and Harriet were dedicated to ending slavery and gave food, clothing, shelter, and any needed supplies to many fleeing slaves. The shop was part of the Underground Railroad, a network of secret places that hid black slaves to help them escape from the United States to Canada.

Abraham Shadd was known as a "conductor" (a person who was important in organizing and helping travelers of the Underground Railroad), and the Shadd home was called a "station." He and Harriet were very brave because helping slaves escape was illegal and the penalties were harsh. They were active "abolitionists," people who wanted to rid the country of slavery; they risked the safety of their family to help people escape. Abraham also wrote for a newspaper called *The Liberator* and in 1838 became president of the National Convention for the Improvement of Free People of Color. He encouraged education and equality. Mary's parents were always very open with their children about the need to fight racism. Mary saw a lot of frightened faces and heard a lot of frightening stories about the treatment of black slaves. She knew her main goal in life would be to fight for liberty.

Black people were not allowed to go to school in Delaware when Mary was growing up, but her parents wanted their children to have an education. When Mary was ten, the Shadds moved to West Chester, Pennsylvania, where there was no such law. Mary went to a school run by Quakers, a religious group and one of the first groups to speak out against slavery. She studied there for the next six years and discovered she had a special gift for language.

Mary knew how lucky she, a black girl, was to get an education. She couldn't wait to start making a difference and opened her own school for black children when she was only sixteen. Her students loved her; she made every subject interesting with her enthusiastic way of talking. Over the next several years, wherever black teachers were needed, Mary went. She taught in Delaware, Pennsylvania, New Jersey, and New York City.

Teaching and travel exposed Mary to many new ideas. In 1849, she felt inspired to share them with others. She wrote her first twelve-page pamphlet, called "Hints to the Colored People of the North." She told people the way to improve the situation of black people was to reject material things, to create rather than buy, and to manage money responsibly. She wrote about independence and confidence. It was the beginning of Mary's career as a bold and clear communicator. Her pamphlet was a success, and she began to write regular newspaper articles. Her views were not always popular, but she was never afraid to express them. She still loved teaching, but more and more she realized the importance of having a strong public voice.

> Mary believed it was important to always work hard and keep trying. "It is better to wear out, than to rust out," she said.

It was a dangerous time for black people in the United States. Under the law, slaves were considered the property of their masters, who felt they had the right to reclaim human beings, like lost objects. To make things even worse, in 1850, the United States passed a law called the Fugitive Slave Act. This allowed slaveholders to track down black people who had once been slaves, whether they were now free or not, and take them back to work.

To avoid slavery, thousands of black people, even more than ever before, escaped to Canada. Canada was not a perfect country, but at least the government had outlawed all slavery as of August 1, 1834. Mary knew that those who immigrated to Canada would need teachers, so in 1851, she moved across the border from Detroit and settled in Windsor, Ontario.

After much discussion with refugee families, Mary decided to open a school. She was encouraged by Henry Bibb, who owned a newspaper called the *Voice of the Fugitive*, and his wife, Mary Bibb, who owned a school nearby. The Bibbs and Mary agreed on many issues regarding freedom, but there were many areas in which they disagreed. Mary's vision of education was special for its time. She wanted schools to be integrated, where all children, black or white, were welcome. The Bibbs wanted schools to be segregated, to be either for black people only or for white people only. Mary argued that all colors had to learn to get along together if they wanted to make progress. She once wrote that her goal was "to get an honest living by teaching persons who have not had opportunities afforded to them."

Mary opened her school and worked long hours. She taught thirteen children by day and held night classes for eleven adults. Everyone was eager to learn, but Mary would have enjoyed it more if the school was not so poorly funded. The building was called the "Old Barracks" and was very drafty and dirty. Many students had colds in the winter and cholera in the summer. To keep the school going, Mary charged each student thirty-seven cents a month for tuition and received a bit of money from the American Missionary Association (AMA).

Mary didn't tell anyone the AMA supported the school. She was afraid students would stop paying their fees and she would have to close down. Henry Bibb, who still did not agree with Mary's integrationist ideas, falsely wrote in his newspaper that she was getting extra money and keeping it for herself. He also disagreed with the opinions Mary expressed in her 1852 forty-four-page pamphlet, "Notes of Canada West." In the pamphlet, Mary tried to convince black people to move to Canada because it had more land, jobs, and integrated schools. Henry's newspaper wrote stories about why Canada was not a good place and why segregation should remain.

Everyone who read Henry's newspaper or Mary's articles knew about the disagreement between the two. Because Henry was a man, readers took him more seriously and were not shocked when he insulted a woman who did not agree with him. In one of his columns, he compared Mary to the biblical snake that tempted Eve. The public was more shocked by Mary, who addressed Henry's attacks with a blunt honesty that women didn't often use.

Mary soon grew tired of the feud and writing articles

A PLEA FOR EMIGRATION;

OR,

NOTES OF CANADA WEST,

IN ITS

MORAL, SOCIAL, AND POLITICAL ASPECT:

WITH

SUGGESTIONS RESPECTING MEXICO, WEST INDIES,
AND VANCOUVER'S ISLAND,

FOR THE

INFORMATION OF COLORED EMIGRANTS.

BY MARY A. SHADD.

DETROIT:
PRINTED BY GEORGE W. PATTISON.
1852.

"Notes of Canada West," dated 1852, was one of Mary's pamphlets. Mary Ann Shadd Cary was a prolific writer who worked for equal rights for women and black people.

for other newspapers. She wanted to start her own newspaper as a way to communicate her opinions about abolition, education, moral values, and other topics to members of the black community. A friend of hers, Reverend Samuel Ringgold Ward, was a well-known activist and speaker on anti-slavery issues. Mary asked him to help her start a newspaper she would call the *Provincial Freeman*. He agreed, although his biggest contribution was his famous name. It was not known at the time, because many people did not believe a woman was smart enough to run a newspaper, but Mary did most of the work. She thought up story ideas and wrote articles. She read letters from readers and edited the text. The paper did well, and had subscribers from across Canada and the United States.

The first issue of the *Provincial Freeman* came out in March 1853, making Mary the first black woman in North America to edit and publish a newspaper. She proudly told people she had finally "broken the editorial ice." Her writing style was like her teaching—never dull. She was an opinionated person and loved to make her readers think and debate. She wrote a lot about teaching the black community to stand up for itself, and the newspaper's motto was "Self-Reliance is the True Road to Independence." She went on business trips across the United States to sell subscriptions, sometimes giving speeches in states where slavery was still permitted.

The Provincial Freeman was a newspaper devoted to issues important to Mary Ann Shadd Cary. Despite doubts of the ability of a woman to run a newspaper, Mary did most of the work.

In January 1856, Mary married Thomas Cary, a black activist and longtime friend with three children, who owned a barbershop in Toronto. She did not allow marriage to disrupt her work. In spite of the open disapproval of many people, she continued to travel and raise money for the *Freeman* while Thomas lived in Toronto. Together, they had two children, a girl named Sarah and a boy named Linton. Linton was born in 1860, just a few months after Thomas died. Mary was left with three stepchildren and two infants to raise by herself. The situation was daunting, but Mary knew she could do it.

In fact, Mary's courage was once a newspaper headline. She saved a young black boy from being sold into slavery by literally grabbing him from the kidnapper's arms. Angered by the injustice, she ran to the courthouse and rang the bell as loud as she could to wake the townspeople to tell them what had happened.

When the Civil War began in 1861, Mary moved to Indiana to work as a recruiter for the Union army. It was a high position, especially for a woman. Mary may have been the only paid woman recruiter in the country, while others were volunteers.

After the war, Mary went to teach in Washington, D.C. She moved her family there and taught in schools for former slaves. She also was asked to attend a convention of the Colored National Labor Union, where she gave a speech about women's roles in the labor movement and encouraged women to learn skilled trades.

In 1869, Mary enrolled at Howard University Law School. One of the first black female law students in the country, Mary kept up an exhausting schedule, attending evening classes and teaching school during the day.

The university refused to let her graduate, even though she was fully qualified because the idea of a woman lawyer

Charlotte Ray was the first female African-American lawyer in the United States. She applied to law school under her initials, C.E. Ray, because the university would not admit women. She earned her law degree, and passed the bar exam in 1872.

seemed too crazy to the men who ran the school. Mary refused to back down and fought the sexual discrimination until finally, in 1883, the school granted her what she had earned, her bachelor of laws (L.L.B.) degree. Again, she was a pioneer in her field as one of the first black women to receive the degree. She was sixty years old.

Mary's courage and interest in justice made her a good lawyer. She worked mostly on smaller cases, and she didn't make much money, but she did make a difference in the lives of her clients. She remained especially interested in helping women, and in 1880, started an organization to help black women budget their money, learn to invest wisely, and therefore be empowered by financial security. It was called the Colored Women's Progressive Franchise Association (CWPFA). She also campaigned to allow women the right to vote.

In 1893, Mary Ann Shadd Cary died, leaving behind a long list of great achievements and important written works. Throughout her life, she was many things: teacher, feminist, writer, publisher, activist, and lawyer. Each role she took involved communicating her thoughts, and she was never afraid to express them. In a society where women were not supposed to have careers, independence, or their own ideas, Mary had all these things and never thought it should be otherwise. Some have called her a rebel, which she was; she was also a fearless leader who paved the way for all those who would follow.

Chapter 4
Emily Murphy
1868–1933

"You must learn to act like a lady." Emily Ferguson heard these words from her mother every day when she was growing up, but she couldn't bring herself to obey. If being a lady meant sitting quietly, as still as a statue, Emily wanted no part of it. She hated being told how to act and was determined to grow up to be a great woman on her own terms.

Emily was born on March 14, 1868, in Ontario, Canada, and had four brothers and one sister. All the Ferguson children were spirited and full of mischief. They would drive their horse-drawn carriage through town at top speed, where they were known as the "young Ferguson devils." Emily never wanted to practice the piano and got scolded for doing somersaults on the couch and stealing apples from the neighbor's trees. Alone in front of the mirror, she pretended she was a famous actress named Rachel.

Maybe the children misbehaved because their parents, Isaac and Emily, were very proper people. They served tea in fancy cups and entertained important guests. Isaac was a successful businessman who had high hopes that his sons would become people of high standing just like him, lawyers or politicians. Emily was treated much like her brothers. She had to gather firewood and do yard work, but she was expected to marry and have children. Law and politics were no place for a lady.

Although Emily was not headed for a career, her father insisted that she get the best education. She started school in her hometown of Cookstown, Ontario, and then boarded at Bishop Strachan private school in Toronto. For the first few months, Emily was homesick and cried every night. She soon came to like her school, however, and her older brothers, Tom and Gowan, took her out on weekends. She told them about playing tennis and learning about plants. She told them that her teachers said that she had a great memory and she could recite entire poems by heart.

Arthur Murphy, who wanted to become a minister, took an interest in Emily. They went on day trips together. Whenever she wrote him a letter, she included a pressed flower. Her brothers helped them keep the relationship secret. Arthur was eleven years older than Emily and her parents wouldn't have approved. "Hurry up and grow so I can marry you," Arthur joked. And that's just what happened on August 23, 1887, five months after Emily turned nineteen.

Going from student to minister's wife was not easy. In her new role, Emily had to be serious and set an example for people much older than herself. She did her best. She studied the Bible, played the organ at church, and joined ladies' clubs. But Emily could never force herself to be proper all the time. She loved to laugh, and the smallest thing gave her the giggles. Once, she burst out laughing in the middle of Arthur's sermon when she thought of a funny joke.

The Murphys had three daughters and a loving marriage. Although she was very busy, Emily wrote in her diary every day. Her writing was a great comfort because Arthur's job caused the family to move often. It was hard starting over, again and again. In 1898, they moved to England where Emily wrote her first book, *Impressions of Janey Canuck Abroad*, which criticized British society with humor.

> At the end of the nineteenth century, the British stereotyped Canadians as rude, rough people who lived in the bush. They thought it was funny to call Canadians "Johnny Canuck." Emily Murphy chose her pen name, Janey Canuck, to make fun of this idea.

When the family returned to Toronto a year later, Emily's career as an author took off. She wrote book reviews and magazine articles about women's issues. *Janey Canuck* was published in 1901. When Arthur got sick with typhoid fever, Emily supported the family with her writing. When her youngest daughter, Doris, died of diphtheria, writing helped her get through her grief.

The family needed a fresh start to escape the sadness of Doris's death. They moved west to Swan River, Manitoba. After Toronto, the Murphys could not believe how small the town was. It didn't even have a hospital. Emily was outraged. What were Swan River residents supposed to do if they got sick? She had just seen her husband though serious illness and lost a child. She would not live through that again. Emily wrote letter after letter to the government, and won her case. When the hospital was built, Emily became president of the hospital board. She also reviewed over twenty books a month for the *Winnipeg Tribune* and wrote another book, *Janey Canuck in the West.*

The family then moved to Edmonton, where Emily was a bit of a celebrity because of the Janey Canuck adventures. She was invited to many parties and lunches, but her favorite thing to do was to visit women who lived on farms. Their husbands controlled every part of their lives, from property to money to legal custody of the children. Her conversations with them opened Emily's eyes to the unfair situation of rural women.

Emily researched the law and learned how the government worked. She watched the legislature in session so that she would be prepared to argue her case. She stopped politicians on the street to tell them about the bill she wanted to pass to help married women.

The first time Emily spoke to the House of Assembly in 1910, her demands were rejected. Word spread of the event and fellow writers and journalists wrote articles supporting her. It was such big news that the new law, called the Dower Act, was passed in Canada in 1911. Married women were now entitled to one-third of their husbands' estates. It was a step forward in women's rights. After that, whenever male politicians saw Emily walking down the street, they'd say, "Here comes trouble." They knew she was a fighter.

After one victory, Emily saw the good that women could accomplish and worked for other causes. She wanted protection for women and children. She wanted prisoners and mental patients to be treated with dignity. Of course her writing was still important and she produced two more books: *Open Trails* in 1912, and *Seeds of Pine* in 1914.

Emily joined women's groups and met others who wanted to make changes, like the famous author and suffragist Nellie McClung. They campaigned hard to get Alberta women the right to vote. They presented petitions and refused to give up. On February 24, 1916, Alberta women were legally allowed to vote and run in federal elections.

One very troubling issue was the way women were treated in court, especially suspected prostitutes. The judge, lawyers, and jury were all men who often thought details of these cases were not appropriate for "ladies" to hear. Sometimes women watching the proceedings were thrown out of court because the lawyers did not want to discuss serious matters in "mixed company." The local Council of Women asked Emily what she thought they could do. She came up with a brilliant idea. Why not have separate courts for women? This would mean big changes in the legal system. At that time, all judges were men. In fact, there had never been a woman judge in the entire British Empire.

Knowing that it was probably just the beginning of another long battle, Emily explained her idea to Charles Cross, the Attorney General of Alberta. When she finished

Emily Murphy (second from right) worked hard to unite women of all ages to the cause of equal rights.

speaking, she got the shock of her life. Charles Cross asked her when she would be ready to start. Judges did not need the university degrees and experience they do today, and Emily already had good knowledge of law. So on June 16, 1916, Emily Murphy was sworn in to her new position, becoming the first woman judge, also called a police magistrate, in the British Empire.

At first the job was challenging, or as Emily put it, "as pleasant as running a rapids without a guide." No one knew what to call a female judge. Some people called her "Your Majesty" or "Sir." Everyone had a lot to learn.

One day when she was about to hear a case, the defense lawyer raised an objection. He said Emily did not have the authority to be a judge because, according to the British North America Act, women were not considered "persons," and only persons could be judges. She had never heard this before, so she went on with her work and decided to investigate.

Emily soon learned that the lawyer's objection was based on a technicality. When

This statue of Emily Murphy was erected in Emily Murphy Park in Edmonton. She stands to remind people of what she fought so hard for: equal rights.

the British North America Act referred to many people, it read "persons." When it referred to one, it read "he." Most people knew the word "he" applied to both men and women, but some wanted to take it literally.

The question went all the way to the Supreme Court of Alberta. In 1917, women welcomed the court's final positive decision. The law, like society, was always changing. If women were slowly gaining all the same rights as men, they were indeed "persons" under the law. This was a good start, but it wasn't good enough. Alberta women were recognized; the law needed to recognize all Canadian women as persons.

> Although Emily fought hard for women's right to sit in the Senate, she was never invited to do so herself. Cairine Wilson was the first woman appointed to the Canadian Senate, in 1930.

Emily campaigned to have a woman appointed to the Senate, which had never been done before. All senators had to be considered "qualified persons" under the British North America Act. If the federal government recognized women as persons, they could be senators. But for years, every time a new position in the Senate opened up, a man was chosen.

The next step was to put together a group of women to help take the case to the Supreme Court of Canada. These women would go down in history as the Famous Five: Emily Murphy, Nellie McClung, Irene Parlby, Louise McKinney, and Henrietta Muir Edwards. Their lawyer was Newton Wesley Rowell, who believed in women's rights. A five-week-long debate began. When the judges came back with their verdict on April 24, 1928, everyone was shocked. At the time of Confederation when the law was written, women were not considered persons. It was no different fifty years later, the judges decided.

The women thought it was crazy to have to fight in court—and then lose—over something so simple. Of course women were "persons." They walked and talked and worked just like men. Why was the law telling them differently?

It was not the time to give up. With Emily, it never was. The women took their case to the highest possible court of appeal, the Judicial Committee of the Privy Council in England. They waited and waited and waited. On the morning of October 18, 1929, it was on the front page of the newspapers: The Supreme Court decision was reversed and Canadian women were considered persons. They had won.

In 1931, Emily retired. She was sixty-three years old and had worked hard all her life. She was also suffering from diabetes and found it difficult to get around. Still, she kept up with her writing until the day that she died, October 26, 1933.

Ever since she was a little girl, Emily had always hated acting like a "lady." She felt that being "ladylike" was just a tradition used to keep women from exercising their rights, and she fought it. She was a strong woman who had endless amounts of compassion for others. Just before Emily's coffin was closed at her funeral, two former prostitutes she had helped placed a rose in her casket. It was sealed inside forever. To this day, Emily Murphy touches the lives of all women in Canada, whatever they do and whoever they are: wives, single women, students, factory workers, and businesswomen. Thanks to her courage, the law officially respects women as human beings.

Chapter 5
Thérèse Casgrain
1896–1981

Thérèse Casgrain told her story of being a little girl at the beginning of the twentieth century. In the story she is dressed in her Sunday best, waiting for her governess. Her dress is frilly, her leather shoes are polished to a brilliant shine, and her hair is perfectly curled. Her eyes wander, and she spots one of her favorite things, a mud puddle. Her mother had told her little girls should not get dirty, but it is impossible to resist. She raises her tiny foot and plunges it into the muddy water! She's filthy but happy because sometimes you have to break the rules. Throughout her life, Thérèse would continue to make a splash in all kinds of areas where women were not supposed to be involved.

Thérèse Forget was born on July 10, 1896, in Montreal, Quebec, the daughter of Blanche MacDonald and Rodolphe Forget. At fourteen, Rodolphe had worked in finance and studied at night to become a lawyer. He tried to learn something new every day and thought others should do the same. A successful man, he owned several businesses and worked with companies around the world, something no other French Canadian had done before. In 1904, he was elected to parliament with the Conservative Party.

The Forgets were wealthy. They had nannies, cooks, maids, and gardeners. Blanche gave fancy parties with live music, and their summer home, called Gil'Mont, had sixteen bedrooms. But all this money did not make Thérèse much different from other children. She still got herself in trouble once in awhile. When she was four, Thérèse spit on the head of a maid she did not like. Her mother gathered the whole household together, and Thérèse apologized in front of everyone. Blanche taught her children that everyone deserved respect and they were no better than anyone else.

Because of Rodolphe's work in business and politics, important people often visited. As a little girl, Thérèse loved to sit and listen to their conversations, even if she didn't always understand them.

When she turned eight, Thérèse went away to boarding school at the Convent of the Sacred Heart. At times, she was homesick, but most of the time, she was happy. The nuns were nice, and there were girls to play with. Some of these girls also had fathers in politics and Thérèse remembered that during prayers, the children of Conservatives lit blue candles and the children of Liberals lit red ones. Those were, and still are, the official party colors.

Her parents took Thérèse out of school for a while to accompany the family to Paris, where her father had business. The fifteen-year-old went to the opera, museums, and amusement parks. It was so much fun that she was happy when the trip was extended and the Forgets canceled their boat tickets home. It was lucky they did; the tickets were for the famous luxury ship _Titanic_, which sank on its way to North America.

When Thérèse left the convent, she studied Italian, literature, and music from home. At a fund-raiser dinner, she met Pierre Casgrain, a lawyer. The next day Pierre sent her flowers and started inviting her on dates. They were married on January 19, 1916.

The following year, Pierre entered politics and ran as a Liberal candidate in the riding of Charlevoix. He and Thérèse campaigned all over the riding despite the winter weather. Once, on a boat, the water was so rough that Thérèse was tied down so that she would not fall out. However, all the travel paid off, and Pierre won the election.

Thérèse continued to support Pierre, but was frustrated by the political system. As a woman, she could not vote. The history of women's suffrage (the right to vote) in Quebec is strange. In 1791, Canada was made up of the two regions of Upper and Lower Canada. If they met certain property guidelines, Quebec women could vote in elections. But in 1843, the parliament of United Canada changed the law and took the right away. It would take many years and perseverance by heroic women until the

On April 17, 1985, a thirty-two-cent stamp bearing a picture of Thérèse was issued in her honor by Canada Post, the Canadian post office.

Women's Suffrage Act was passed in 1918 and women could vote in federal elections. However, there was still one problem in Quebec. Although women could vote on the federal level, they were still not allowed to participate in provincial elections.

The situation made no sense to many women in Quebec, including Thérèse. In 1921, French and English women of Quebec formed a new bilingual group—the Provincial Suffrage Committee. On behalf of the committee, Thérèse gave speeches to the premier of Quebec, Louis-Alexandre Taschereau. All he said was, "If the women of Quebec ever get the right to vote, they will not have got it from me."

Thérèse became president of the Provincial Suffrage Committee in 1928, which changed its name to the League for Women's Rights that year. At the time, feminists faced infuriating remarks from men, such as, "The least the ladies can do is leave politics to the gentlemen." A married mother of four, Thérèse easily disproved the ideas that suffragettes were bitter, childless man-haters. The League and other women's organizations fought for the vote until finally, in 1940, they won.

Thérèse knew a lot about political life and had discovered, in 1921, that she liked it. During the reelection campaign in the Charlevoix riding, when Pierre was to give a speech, he fell ill and could not get out of bed. Thérèse stood up in front of a crowd of a thousand people, explained why Pierre was not there, and delivered the speech herself. She did such a good job that Pierre was reelected.

For years to come, Thérèse kept that moment in the back of her mind as her interest in politics grew. She wanted to be more than a voter; she wanted to be a candidate. When she went with Pierre to the homes of other politicians, the wives—except Thérèse—played cards while the men discussed issues. Thérèse did not want to play cards; she wanted to talk politics.

Thérèse knew running to be a member of Parliament would be difficult, but she wanted to break people's prejudices against women. She ran as an independent Liberal candidate in 1942 in Charlevoic-Saguenay, the same district her father and husband had represented. There were four male opponents, who were determined not to be defeated by a woman. One newspaper editor wrote that Thérèse should quit: "Let her cook, sew, embroider, read, card wool, play bridge—anything other than persist in her dangerous role."

She campaigned everywhere. The riding was 700 miles (1,127 km) long, and she traveled by car, truck, train, boat, and canoe to talk to the voters. She traveled more than her male opponents did and in the end came in second place. It was a close race, and Thérèse felt proud to have done so well. She would persevere. Throughout her political career, she ran in nine elections and while she never won, the defeats never stood in her way.

After a few years with the Liberals, Thérèse decided the party was not right for her. The men did not make her feel welcome, and they knew Thérèse would never change her opinion just to fit in. The beliefs of the Co-operative Commonwealth Federation (CCF) party, known today as the

In 1979, Thérèse Casgrain, founder of the Quebec League for Human Rights, accepted the Governor General's Award in recognition of her work for women's rights.

New Democratic Party (NDP), were closer to her own. The CCF party supported family allowances, unemployment insurance, and old-age pensions. Thérèse thought the CCF believed money should be used to help people, not just to make more money. On December 11, 1946, she joined the CCF. They were a small party and they didn't have a lot of resources, but with them Thérèse felt at home right away. At first, she worried that her husband might not support her— he was a longtime Liberal. But he appreciated that her opinions were different and admired her independent spirit.

Two years later, the CCF elected Thérèse vice-president of the Quebec branch. She was sent as a delegate to an international socialist convention in Germany, and while she was away, the CCF elected her leader. She was the first woman in Quebec to lead a political party.

As a girl, Thérèse had read a book called *Around the World in Eighty Days*, but never thought she would be lucky enough to have such an adventure. It began in 1956, when she attended a meeting of the Socialist Nations of Asia in India. The Taj Mahal and the bluest ocean she'd ever seen only marked the start of her trip. She traveled all over the world on behalf of the CCF, to Thailand, China, Japan, and Burma (today officially called Myanmar). She not only visited tourist attractions but also factories to see what the working conditions were like. She discussed social problems such as poverty and education with world leaders.

Thérèse's greatest wish was for world peace. She hated the thought of innocent people dying because governments could not get along. In 1961, she founded the Quebec branch of the Voice of Women and became its president. The group campaigned against nuclear war and attended conferences in Italy, Russia, and Finland to work for international disarmament. Along with other women, she presented a petition to the NATO defense ministers opposing the building of nuclear weapons. NATO security feared these women were there to make trouble and threw them in jail. They had no food, heat, or water but spent the time singing and talking until their release.

This 1985 Canadian stamp features Thérèse Casgrain. She was also commemorated in 2004 on the back of the new Canadian $50 bill.

Poverty was another important cause for Thérèse, and she worked long and hard to improve the lives of working people. As a young woman, she was a member of the Commission for Minimum Wages, which worked to make sure jobs paid people enough to live. She met women who worked for ten hours a day in factories but could barely afford to feed their families. Country schoolteachers were also struggling. Some only earned $150 a year. Because she believed that people deserve quality products when they spend their hard-earned money, Thérèse became president of the Canadian Consumers Association of Quebec in 1969. She led their campaign to create the position of Minister of Consumer Affairs.

On October 8, 1970, Prime Minister Pierre Elliott Trudeau called Thérèse at her home. He offered her a seat in the Senate. At first she hesitated. She knew senators had to retire at age seventy-five and she was already seventy-four. But she thought about all the good things she might accomplish and accepted the prime minister's proposal.

As soon as she was sworn in, Thérèse Casgrain jumped right into the debates. She made sure the other senators were aware of women's issues. She dealt with the report of the Royal Commission on the Status of Women. She was outraged that women only made up 1 percent of the

Canadian government, and in Quebec, were not allowed to sit on juries. They still had to fight for equal rights every day.

After nine months on the Senate, Thérèse retired. But she continued to work with women's groups and to speak out against war. Meanwhile, more and more organizations were recognizing the value of her work. In 1967, she became a member of the Order of Canada. That same year, the Council of Jewish Women of Canada named her "Woman of the Century" in Quebec, and the Société de criminologie du Canada honored her for "defense of human rights and the ideals of justice in our society." A total of twelve universities gave her honorary degrees.

Thérèse Forget Casgrain was born with advantages many people never have. She came from a wealthy background and was well known in her community. She could have stayed home and lived comfortably, without worries. Instead, she took an interest in her country and in her world, especially in the injustices people faced. She was a longtime leader in the peace movement. She fought for justice in the workplace. Refusing to believe women were anything less than men, she devoted her life to the struggle for women's rights and introduced feminist ideas to those who had never heard of them before. For Thérèse, politics was a way to reach people and change their lives for the better. Her autobiography is called *A Woman in a Man's World*, and she spent her entire life working to make a world in which everyone felt equal.

Chapter 6

Golda Meir

1898–1978

"The thing that mattered most in my life was that if a thing had to be done, you don't waste time...You just do it." Golda Meir spoke these words long before a sportswear company used them as its slogan. As a woman of action, there was no problem she would not tackle in her personal or political life. She certainly was one of the most determined women of the twentieth century.

Golda was born in Kiev, Russia, on May 3, 1898. She was the middle child in a family of three girls (Sheyna was older, Clara younger) of parents Moshe and Blume Mabovitch. Being Jewish, the family faced a lot of discrimination. Moshe worked as a carpenter and was often cheated out of his wages. He would build furniture for customers who would sometimes refuse to pay him once they realized he was Jewish. No matter how hard he worked, anti-Semitism (hatred of Jews) kept Moshe and his family in deep poverty.

It was not just being poor that made Golda's childhood difficult. As a Jew, she lived in fear of pogroms, attacks by angry mobs on Jewish people. Golda always remembered huddling with other children listening in terror to the sound of soldiers on horseback.

When Golda was five years old, her father sailed across the ocean to live in Milwaukee, Wisconsin. There, he worked so that he could save enough money to send for the rest of the family, which he did in 1906. In the United States, they hoped they could live in peace, away from the violence and persecution.

Life was much different in their new country. Blume opened a small store in the front room of the family's house, and Golda helped out by working there before and after school. Golda wanted to be useful, but she did not want to be late for school every morning (which she was) because she was watching the store. She loved classes and did not want to miss a single minute, but her parents didn't understand. They felt a girl's priority should be marriage, not education. But Golda was a big thinker early on.

Golda's young mind never stopped buzzing with ideas. When she was in fourth grade, she decided that it was unfair that children had to pay for their own schoolbooks when many of their parents were poor and could not afford the money. Without any help, she organized a town meeting, renting a room and sending out invitations. Dozens of people showed up to hear the eleven-year-old give a speech asking for donations. When Golda gave her speech, she didn't even use notes, she simply spoke from her heart. By the end of the night, she had raised enough money to buy the needed textbooks for every child in the school.

Golda Meir's story has inspired and entertained. There are three plays written about her: *Golda* and *Golda's Balcony* by William Gibson and *An Evening with Golda Meir* by Renee Taylor. There was also a television mini-series starring Ingrid Bergman, entitled *A Woman Named Golda.*

When Golda could no longer stand fighting with her parents about school (she wanted to go on to high school and they didn't think it was important), she moved to Denver, Colorado, to stay with her sister, Sheyna, who was now married. Sheyna was involved with a group of young Russian immigrants who had passionate discussions about politics, philosophy, revolution, and Zionism, the creation of a state for Jewish people in Palestine where they could live together in peace. Golda often went to these meetings and considered this period the real beginning of her education. Fascinated by these new ideas, she quickly became an active Zionist. Near the end of high school, she returned to her parents' house and continued spreading the message to American Jews. She got her teaching certificate, but instead took a job with a socialist Zionist group because the cause was so important to her. She even stood on a soapbox outside synagogues or on street corners and gave speeches, never needing notes.

While she lived in Denver, Golda met Morris Meyerson. He wasn't very political but knew a lot about art and music. He wanted a quiet, traditional family life, while Golda's dream was to move to a kibbutz (a large farm in Palestine where many families live together and share the workload). Despite their differences, the two liked each other instantly and were married in 1917.

In 1921, Golda and Morris migrated to a kibbutz near Nazareth in Palestine. At first, it was hard for Golda to fit in with the others. They saw her as the "American girl" and thought she would be too accustomed to luxury to do hard work. Of course Golda was determined to prove them wrong and participated in all the work, including building houses, paving roads, and cooking.

Although Golda enjoyed her new life among people who shared her Zionist ideas, Morris became very ill and was unable to work with the rest of the group. They left the kibbutz after three years and moved to a two-room apartment in Tel Aviv, Israel. Jobs were very hard to find, and they had little money. It became even more difficult once they had children—a son, Menachem, and a daughter, Sarah—and Golda did other people's laundry to help support her family.

Golda Meir and her husband, Morris Meyerson, pose for a portrait shortly before their wedding in 1917. Golda changed her last name to Meir, which means "to burn brightly," in 1956.

Things got better in 1928 when she got a job as secretary of the Women's Labor Council of the Histadrut, a Zionist labor group. She was thrilled to be once again doing what she loved, but the job involved a lot of travel throughout Palestine and some to the United States and Canada, so she was often away from her family. Morris found it difficult to get used to her new lifestyle. The two eventually separated but remained good friends.

Golda flourished with the Histadrut, and by 1936 was head of its political department.

Her talent for public speaking, her experience with fund-raising, and her ability to speak fluent Yiddish, Hebrew, and English made her extremely good at her job. As if she was not busy enough, she also helped found a new political party, Mapai.

Adolf Hitler, dictator of Nazi Germany, hated Jewish people and wanted to rid the world of their entire race. During World War II, he sent millions to concentration camps, where they were tortured and murdered. All over Europe, Jews lived in constant fear of being sent to these camps and looked to escape to safer countries, but almost no country would let them in. Palestine, which was ruled by Britain at the time, would have been a good homeland for the refugees. Instead of agreeing to allow a large number of Jewish people to migrate to Palestine, the British government made a law severely restricting the number of Jews who were allowed to enter. Golda feared for the lives of the persecuted and secretly helped many Jews escape to Palestine.

After the atrocities of World War II, Golda was more determined than ever to see her Zionist dream come to life. The British arrested many Jewish leaders who supported independence, but Golda was not afraid. She became head of the Political Bureau of the Jewish Agency in Jerusalem in 1946 and was in charge of helping survivors of Nazi concentration camps settle in the new land. In 1947, the United Nations finally announced that Palestine should be split into two separate states, one Arab and one Jewish, and

> "[Israeli prime minister] David Ben-Gurion described me as the 'only man' in his cabinet ... obviously he thought that this was the greatest possible compliment that could be paid a woman. I very much doubt that any man would have been flattered if I had said about him that he was the 'only woman' in the government!"
>
> —GOLDA MEIR

Prime Minister of Israel, Golda Meir, speaks from her podium in 1970. She became prime minister after her predecessor suffered a heart attack.

on May 14, 1948, Israel's Declaration of Independence was signed. Golda could not have been happier as she put her signature on the document.

However, the Arab nations were not happy and immediately began to bomb the Jewish state. In order to defend themselves, Israel's army needed money and Prime Minister David Ben-Gurion sent Golda to raise funds in the United States. In only six weeks of speeches and touring, she raised $50 million. Golda then became the first Israeli ambassador to Moscow and stayed there for a year.

Returning to Israel, she took the government position of minister of labor and housing. Among its many challenges was the building of houses for the hundreds of thousands of Jewish people who came from other countries, as there were no longer any limits on how many could enter. During this time, Golda also ran in an election for the mayor of Tel Aviv, but lost.

In 1956, Golda, along with other government officials, decided to take a Hebrew name. Meyerson was changed to Meir, which means "to burn brightly." The same year, she was also appointed foreign minister, making her world-renowned as one of Israel's most important political figures. She traveled to Africa and Asia, where she met with political officials and used her own experience to teach countries about how to build an independent nation.

In 1963, Golda was diagnosed with cancer. Because she had always kept up her image as a strong, fearless leader, she did not want it to be publicly known that she was ill. She took a short break from politics in 1965 to regain her strength. Besides being sick, a lifetime of hard work had left her exhausted. She also wanted to experience a quiet life and spend some time with her grandchildren. Her temporary retirement did not last long, and after a year, she became head of the political party Mapai and was again working on labor issues. A second attempt to retire in 1968 was also short-lived.

> Sirimavo Bandaranaike became prime minister of Sri Lanka in 1960, and Indira Gandhi became prime minister of India in 1966. Golda was the third woman prime minister. Since then, many other women around the world have held the title.

In 1969, the prime minister of Israel, Levi Eshkol, died of a heart attack, and Golda became the new prime minister, the third woman in the world to hold the title. Battles between Israel and Arab nations still were underway and Israel was suffering. Even though Golda did not consider fighting a solution, she often saw no other alternative and refused to allow

Golda Meir was commemorated on the one thousand shekalim (the plural of shekel) bill in 1983. Because of inflation, the currency of Israel (the old skekel) was replaced by the new shekel in 1985.

her nation to be threatened. Known for being a tough, confident person and doing what she believed was necessary, she went to Washington to ask for weapons and financial aid.

In 1973, as Yom Kippur approached, the Israeli intelligence heard that Egyptian and Syrian forces were planning to attack. Yom Kippur, or the "Day of Atonement," is a sacred day for the Jewish people, observed by fasting, doing no work, and praying in synagogue. Although Golda did not usually shy away from conflict when she thought it was necessary, she could not believe there would be a battle during such a holy time. She decided not to send out troops, but on October 6, Egypt and Syria did indeed start a battle. Although Golda ordered the military to fight back as soon as the bombs fell, many blamed her for the country's lack of preparation. Others supported their prime minister because Israel won the battle with help from the United States. The Yom Kippur War was the most controversial moment of Golda's career. She had underestimated her opponents and was forced to resign.

Leaving politics was not necessarily a bad thing for Golda. For the past few years, she had secretly been undergoing radiation treatment for her cancer, and she felt it was time to step back and look after herself. She wrote her autobiography, *My Life*, published in 1975. She also spent more time with her family, and enjoyed being a grandmother.

Golda Meir died on December 8, 1978. She is remembered internationally as a woman with many sides. She was an exciting speaker, a take-charge person, a tough world leader, and a grandmother who loved to cook. No matter what stood in her way, whether poverty, illness, war or prejudice, she fought back. Like the light of a single candle on a dark night, her spirit burns brightly.

Every day, millions of people ride the bus for school, work, shopping, or from one city or town to another. Some people like to sit at the front to see the road ahead. Others prefer the back to see the other passengers. In the 1950s, Rosa Parks rode a bus to work five days a week. Even though black people had supposedly been equal citizens for almost a hundred years, the law did not allow her to choose her seat. In fact, she and other black people were not allowed to do many things because of the color of their skin. Rosa Parks, known as the "mother of the civil rights movement," is one woman who put the wheels of change in motion.

Rosa McCauley was born on February 3, 1913. Her father was a carpenter and worked in different towns. He was often away from home. Rosa and her little brother Sylvester were raised by their mother and their grandparents. They all lived together on a farm in Pine Level, Alabama.

The farm kept Rosa busy all day. She fed the chickens and weeded the vegetable gardens. When work time was over, she played with her brother and went fishing.

Nighttime was scary. A group of white men called the Ku Klux Klan (KKK) terrorized black people. The KKK wore robes and hoods over their faces. They killed black people and burned down their houses. Rosa's grandfather didn't sleep much. He stayed awake with a shotgun at his side to protect his family in case the KKK showed up.

Grandfather told great stories and he spoke with feeling, but the stories were not always happy. He had grown up on a plantation, and because he was a black man, the white plantation owners hit him, made him do back-breaking work, and fed him scraps. Rosa's grandfather wanted his grandchildren to be strong and never let anyone treat them badly.

Her grandfather said an educated person got respect. But women in Alabama, especially black women, often did not go past sixth grade in school. They had to work to earn money for their families. They also were only allowed to do certain jobs. The most common was domestic work, cleaning houses for wealthy white people.

Rosa's mom took her father's advice. She studied hard and became a teacher, but even with her education, there were limitations. Black teachers could only teach black children and were not paid as much as white teachers.

At age six, Rosa started school. She was smaller than the other children and often sick with tonsillitis. She could not run fast or catch a ball. She played "ring games" like Ring Around the Roses. By the time she started first grade, Rosa already knew how to read; her mother had taught her early. Rosa loved fairy tales like *Little Red Riding Hood* and Mother Goose nursery rhymes. She was the best reader in her class.

> "To this day, I believe we are here on the planet Earth to live, grow up, and do what we can to make this world a better place for all people to enjoy freedom."
>
> —ROSA PARKS

Small and spunky, Rosa wasn't afraid to stand up for herself. Once, a white boy on roller skates tried to push her, and she pushed him right back. The boy's mother told Rosa she could have her arrested, but Rosa didn't care. She didn't like being pushed.

Schools were segregated, meaning that black children and white children had separate schools. The school Rosa attended was made of wood, built and paid for by people in the black community. When it was chilly, a parent would deliver a wagon of firewood. The bigger boys carried the wood and tended the fire. Black children walked to school. There were sixty students in one room with only one teacher. The children went to school for five months, then worked in the fields for the rest of the year.

The local school for white children was made of brick and built with money from state taxpayers, who were both white and black. The state heated the building and made repairs. The school year was nine months long. White children also had buses to take them to and from school. Sometimes they would throw garbage out the bus windows at black children they passed on the road. When Rosa and her brother saw a bus coming, they hid in the fields until it

A man drinks from a "colored" drinking fountain in Oklahoma City in 1938. This type of treatment was due to Jim Crow laws, which mandated segregation in all public facilities.

passed. Many white children learned from their parents to treat black people badly.

Not all white people in Pine Level were cruel, but it was hard to understand why so many were. Rosa didn't know the word "racism" or even how bad the problem was until she went to Montgomery to go to school. She was eleven and her old school only went up to sixth grade. In the city, there was more segregation. White people and black people had separate libraries, hotels, restaurants, churches, and elevators. Water fountains were labeled "White" and "Colored."

Montgomery Industrial School was a private school, and all students paid tuition to attend. Rosa's mother saved money from her teaching job so that her daughter could go. Alice White was the principal, and all the teachers were white women. Some people didn't like white people educating black children. Twice, Miss White's school was burned down in violent protests. Rosa was a good student, and Miss White's school gave children confidence. It reminded Rosa of what her grandfather and mother had taught her, that she deserved respect and could achieve any goal she wanted in life. A person's skin color didn't matter.

When she reached eleventh grade, Rosa's grandmother and mother got sick. It made her sad, but Rosa had to drop out of school to care for her family.

A barber named Raymond Parks entered Rosa's life when she was eighteen. He went to Rosa's house and took her for drives. Raymond told Rosa about a group that he belonged to called the National Association for the Advancement of Colored People (NAACP). They worked on issues like helping black people vote and defending wrongly accused prisoners. Raymond always stood up for his rights and the rights of all black people. Because of his courage and intelligence, Rosa fell in love. They married in December

In this 1956 photo, black citizens sit at the back of the bus. In order to enforce segregation, many bus drivers carried guns.

"People always say that I didn't give up my seat because I was tired, but that isn't true. I was not tired physically...No, the only tired I was, was tired of giving up."

Rosa Parks prepares for her court appearance in the 1956 bus boycott trial. The boycott started on the day Rosa was fined for not giving up her seat to a white man.

1932, and moved to Montgomery. Three years later, Rosa got her high school diploma.

Over the next several years, Rosa volunteered with the NAACP. She became its secretary in 1943. An excellent reader and writer, she enjoyed composing letters for the association. Most important, she kept track of all reported cases of discrimination. By the late 1940s, she was also adviser to the NAACP Youth Council. Working with young people and all their fresh ideas was her favorite position.

When she wasn't volunteering, Rosa worked full-time as a dressmaker in a department store. It wasn't her dream job, but discrimination made it hard for black women to find work. From Monday to Friday, she rode a city bus to the store and back. Public buses were segregated like everything else. The first ten rows were for white people, the back rows for black people. Bus drivers had "police power" to enforce the segregation, and some even carried guns. If a white person got on a bus and the first ten rows were full, the black people in the next row back had to give up their seats for the white person.

> Rosa Parks was not the first black woman to refuse to give up her seat on a bus. In 1955, two other women, Claudette Colvin and Louise Smith, refused on separate occasions. Both were arrested and fined.

One bus driver who was particularly racist would not allow Rosa to enter the bus by the front doors. After she had paid, he told her to get off the bus and enter through the back doors. When she tried to argue with him, he grabbed her by the sleeve, forced her off the bus and drove away, leaving Rosa on the curb. She never forgot the hateful look in his eyes. From that day on, if Rosa saw him driving, she waited for the next bus.

After a typical day at work on December 1, 1955, Rosa caught the bus home. Too late she noticed who was driving but she sat down anyway. At the next stop, a white man got on the bus, but the first ten rows were full. The driver turned around and said, "Let me have those seats." The people sitting in the same row as Rosa stood up. She thought about her grandfather and his lessons about deserving respect. She remained seated. The driver said he would have her arrested. Everyone on the bus fell silent. Rosa looked at him and said, "You may do that." The police came and arrested her.

Word of Rosa's arrest spread quickly in the black community. E.D. Nixon, president of the Alabama branch of the NAACP, asked Rosa to fight her case in court and she agreed. Segregation and the humiliation of black people had to stop.

Nixon made big plans. He spoke to Jo Ann Robinson, a member of the Women's Political Council. It was her idea to boycott the buses. Since 70 percent of riders were black, the city would be financially hurt if they banded together. They handed out flyers and talked to everyone they saw. Church ministers, such as Dr. Martin Luther King Jr., told their congregations that on Monday, December 5, no one should ride the buses.

Monday came, and everyone was nervous. Would the boycott work? The first buses rolled down the street, empty. They remained empty all day long. To support Rosa Parks and the anti-segregation campaign, people took taxis or got rides with others. Many people walked to work, which meant getting up earlier and getting home later. It looked like a parade twice a day, with so many people walking along the streets.

Rosa went to the courthouse that same morning with a lawyer named Fred Gray. She paid the fine but said she would appeal the case. Outside, people clapped and cheered at her decision, but it would be a long time before they could really celebrate.

At first, no one knew how long the boycott would last because an appeal can take years. Black people negotiated with the bus company for equal treatment on buses, but the company said no. Some white people were angry about the disruption and yelled at black people waiting for taxis. Black car drivers could not get insurance and were arrested for no reason. Many lost their jobs, including Rosa and Raymond. After three months, the buses stopped running because they had lost so much money. Then, when people across the country followed Montgomery's lead and protested segregation, a nationwide movement for civil rights began.

Rosa's case went all the way to the Supreme Court, the highest court in the United States. The final decision banned segregation on public buses. On December 21, 1956, it was official; the boycott was over. It had lasted thirteen months.

It was a rough year for Rosa. She lost her job, went to court, and received threatening phone calls even after the boycott ended. She moved to Detroit, Michigan, to get away from the spotlight but continued to fight for civil rights by working for a black congressman, John Conyers. She stayed at the job for twenty years and worked to make Martin Luther King Jr. Day a national holiday.

Raymond died in 1977, and ten years later, Rosa started up the Rosa & Raymond Parks Institute for Self Development. It teaches young people how to be leaders and work for their communities. They have a special program, Pathways to Freedom, where children from all racial backgrounds take a bus trip through the United States and Canada, following the Underground Railroad. Rosa often went along on these trips and told her story to young people. In 1988, she went to the Democratic National Convention to support black leader Jesse Jackson in his presidential campaign. At the convention, Jackson presented her as a pioneer of the civil rights movement.

Rosa has been honored and praised all over America, but she was modest about her accomplishments. She said, "I was not the only person involved. I was just one of many who fought for freedom." She was awarded the Presidential Medal of Freedom, the Congressional Gold Medal and the Martin Luther King, Jr. Nonviolent Peace Prize. In December, 2000, Montgomery paid her tribute by opening the Rosa Parks Library and Museum.

Rosa Parks died on October 24, 2005, at the age of 92. After her death, her casket was held in the U.S. Capitol for two days so that the nation could pay their final respects to the woman who left such a mark on this country. Rosa is the only woman, and only the second black person, to lay in honor in the Capitol, an honor usually reserved only for U.S. presidents.

Sometimes the smallest gesture sparks the biggest changes. On that December afternoon in 1955, Rosa Parks had no idea she would inspire millions to fight for what was right. She had no idea staying seated would make her a leader for equality. She had no idea she would become a heroine. Rosa Parks showed us what self-respect and courage can accomplish.

Chapter 8
Wangari Maathai
1940–2011

You probably know that Earth's environment has many problems. Air and water pollution, forests lost because of clear-cutting and the weakening of the ozone layer are just a few we are trying to fix. These are large and serious difficulties, but if everyone helps out, the job is not impossible. Maybe you recycle or turn out the light when you leave a room? Although these are small things, every action makes a difference. Wangari Maathai, an environmentalist and politician, believes this and has proven it is true. What started with a few women planting trees has improved the lives of thousands of African people.

Wangari Maathai (pronounced *wahn-GARH-ee mah-TIE*) was born in Nyeri in the East African country of Kenya on April 1, 1940. She grew up on a farm with her parents, who had five children. Wangari was the oldest and had a lot of responsibilities. Besides caring for her siblings, she worked on the farm, and helped clean the house and grow the crops. Her favorite job was watering the beautiful fig tree that grew in their yard. Her mother did not want her interfering with the tree's natural cycle, so she did not let Wangari touch the tree or pick up its twigs off the ground.

Wangari's ancestors are the Kikuyu community. Wangari believes that if the Kikuyu had a motto, it would be "The sky's the limit." They dream big and Wangari grew up thinking that anything is possible. Her parents taught her the traditional skills of Kikuyu women, like cooking and sewing, but they were different from other parents. They also wanted Wangari to go to school and be independent. They wanted her to see new places. Many children, especially girls, did not go to school. They had to stay at home and help with chores. Wangari was lucky. Without her parents' encouragement, she thinks she would have stayed on the farm forever.

At the age of eight, Wangari started school. Her teachers saw that she was smart and not afraid of hard work. She did well in all her classes, but science was her favorite. Her teachers thought someone like Wangari would be happier at college than on a farm. At the Loreto Girls' School, Wangari's high school, she won a scholarship to study at Mount St. Scholastica College in Atchison, Kansas, and crossed the ocean to the United States. Wangari had always loved plants and animals. She wanted to learn how nature worked, so she got a Bachelor of Science degree in biology.

Wangari was such an enthusiastic student that she did not stop after her first graduation. In 1964, she went to the

University of Pittsburgh. After two more years of study, she became the first woman in eastern and central Africa to earn a master's degree.

Wangari never intended to stay in the United States permanently. In the six years she had lived away from home, she thought about what she would do when she returned. She planned to use what she had learned to make Kenya a better country. She wanted to make a contribution.

It was easy for Wangari to find work in Kenya. She took a job as a research assistant in the department of veterinary medicine at the University of Nairobi. Her education and experience impressed several of her colleagues at the university, including a professor from Germany. Not everyone felt the same way, however.

At the time, the rules for Kenyan women were strict and old-fashioned. Women were supposed to be quiet. They were not supposed to be ambitious or want careers. In the home, the man was the "master" and the woman obeyed. But Wangari had been raised to speak her mind. To many Kenyan men, the idea of a woman professor was new and some did not accept her. They did not take her seriously. Some even called her master's degree a joke, just because she was a woman. But Wangari was tough and said that she had the "skin of an elephant." She kept working and ignored the unjust and cruel things some of the men had said.

In 1971, Wangari became the first woman at the University of Nairobi to earn her Ph.D. As a

> "Others told me that I shouldn't have a career, that I shouldn't raise my voice, that women are supposed to have a master. That I needed to be someone else. Finally I was able to see that if I had a contribution I wanted to make, I must do it, despite what others said. That I was OK the way I was. That it was all right to be strong."
>
> —WANGARI MAATHAI

professor, she gave lectures and was a senior member of the school. She became the first woman Chair of the Department of Veterinary Medicine. Besides her demanding academic career, she also juggled her responsibilities as a wife and mother.

> "I don't really know why I care so much. I just have something inside me that tells me that there is a problem and I have to do something about it."
>
> —WANGARI MAATHAI

Wangari was good at doing research and writing reports, but she felt there was more she could do to make her contribution. In the early 1970s, two things inspired her future work for people and the environment.

The first was when Wangari's husband, a businessman, ran for Parliament. Working with him, she campaigned throughout Nairobi meeting new people and seeing new places. The scenes were often upsetting. Many people could not find jobs. They lived in slums and were starving. Wangari identified with the women who could not feed their children. It hurt her to imagine her own three children starving. Her husband told the poor people he would find them work if he was elected, but his wife took the promise more seriously than he did. She vowed to find a way to better their lives.

The second thing happened when Wangari studied tiny bugs and got a big idea. Certain herds of cattle were dying. She wanted to find out why. At first, the reason seemed to be a kind of tick that spread sickness. Wangari went out into the fields to study the insects, where the real cause was clear; it was the land. There were no trees. There was no clean drinking water or nutritious grass. Wangari studied the situation and found out that three-quarters of Kenya's forests had been cut down in only 150 years, and more trees were being lost every day.

As a biologist, Wangari knew the importance of trees. Leaves make oxygen and provide shade. Roots keep soil moist so that it does not erode. Trees also purify water, making it safe to drink. Fruit from trees give children the vitamins to grow up strong and help all people stay healthy. A tree is also a renewable source of energy. People need firewood to cook meals and build homes, but here some women had to walk as far as 20 miles (30 km) to collect kindling.

Thinking about the problems of poverty, starvation, and the environment, Wangari had an idea. What if people worked planting trees? They could earn money for their families and help save the environment at the same time. Wangari joined the National Council of Women of Kenya (NCWK) and told them about her idea. On Earth Day, June 5, 1977, Wangari's group planted seven *nandi* (flame) trees in a park. Wangari had grown them from seeds in her

The headquarters of the Green Belt Movement can be seen in this picture taken in Nairobi. The initiative gave Wangari Maathai the Nobel Peace Prize in 2004.

Activist Kario Wanae tends to a tree at the Green Belt Movement nursery. In addition to planting trees, the GBM also works to raise awareness about women's rights, civic empowerment, and the environment.

backyard. From those seven trees, a national organization was born. They called themselves the Green Belt Movement (GBM) and believed that women could help solve the environment's problems. At first, the men who worked as government foresters laughed. They said only foresters could plant trees, not women. They said Wangari and the others should give up before they failed. The women did not listen.

The Green Belters grow saplings (young trees) in nurseries. Some trees, like acacias and thorn trees, are for firewood. Others are grown for fruit like bananas, figs, and oranges. GBM gives the saplings to churches, farms, hospitals, or any place that needs them. Ninety percent of Green Belters are women who work part-time to help feed their families. Children are very important to the GBM, too, because they plant trees at school and make it a project to care for them.

The movement grew fast. Soon, thousands of women across Kenya were planting and raising trees with the GBM. By the 1980s, there were six hundred nurseries. When other countries heard about what Kenyan women were doing, they wanted to plant trees, too. Tanzania, Uganda, Malawi, Lesotho, Ethiopia, and Zimbabwe all started their own Green Belt Movement groups.

Wangari was a well-known environmentalist and chairperson of the NCWK. However, some men have problems with strong, successful women, and Wangari's husband was one of those men. He did not want a wife who was more famous than he was, and he did not like that she had her own ideas and was independent. He left her and their three children and filed for divorce. The court papers said he wanted the divorce because Wangari was "too educated, too strong, too successful, too stubborn and too hard to control."

Besides planting new trees, Wangari fought to save existing green spaces. In 1989, Kenya's president Daniel arap Moi planned to build a sixty-two-story skyscraper in Uhuru Park, where many Kenyans went to walk, play, and be with nature. The building would cost $200 million (U.S.), and Kenya was already in debt.

"The world needs leadership that recognizes the need to care for the world beyond local interests and concerns, beyond national and regional borders, beyond race, religion, gender, culture and class."

—WANGARI MAATHAI

Wangari Maathai plants a tree in 1999 at Freedom Corner Uhuru Park in Nairobi, Kenya. The preservation of parks is one of the causes that drove her to founding the GBM.

Wangari wanted to save the park for everyone to enjoy. She saw Nairobi becoming only buildings with no trees. But President Moi wanted a fancy new building. The government said unfair things about Wangari because she was the leader of the protestors. Moi said it was "unimaginable for a woman to challenge or oppose men," and called the GBM "a bunch of angry divorcées." One member of Parliament suggested they put a *salasa* (a curse) on Wangari.

Thanks to her "skin of an elephant," Wangari ignored the insults. So, the government tried other things. They evicted the GBM from its office in a state-owned building. The group made new offices at Wangari's house, and she joked about how she loved having such a big family. But in the end, the skyscraper was not built.

Wangari, Deputy Minister of the Environment, Natural Resources, and Wildlife, speaking at the State House, Nairobi.

Wangari took her environmentalism into politics, and in 1997, she ran against President Moi in the presidential elections. Because she dared to go against Moi's government, Wangari was in danger many times. She was arrested more than once for being a "troublemaker" and was once beaten unconscious by police during protests. Unfortunately, the day

> "We have a special responsibility to the ecosystem of this planet. In making sure that other species survive, we will be ensuring the survival of our own."
> —WANGARI MAATHAI

before the election, a false rumor went around that Wangari had dropped out of the race. She got almost no votes because no one thought she was a candidate.

In 1998, Moi planned to build a group of expensive houses. To do so, he would clear-cut thousands of acres of Kenyan forest. Wangari hated the plans. Most Kenyans could not afford the luxury houses. It was not worth cutting down so many trees. Wangari and a dozen other women planted saplings on the site to protest. Moi sent men with whips, swords, and bows and arrows. The women had only their gardening tools. The men beat Wangari and her helpers with their weapons, forcing them to leave.

In 2002, there were new elections for the president of Kenya and Mwai Kibabi won against Daniel arap Moi. President Kibabi supported the GBM and agreed with many of Wangari's views on the environment, too. Under the new president, Wangari got a seat in the Kenyan parliament. Even better, in 2003, she was named Deputy Minister of the Environment, Natural Resources and Wildlife.

Throughout the 1980s, Wangari was honored with awards such as the Woman of the World Award and the Right Livelihood Award. In 1991, she received the Goldman

Environmental Prize and the Africa Prize for Leadership for the Sustainable End to Hunger.

Today, the Green Belt Movement has about six thousand nurseries. Over one hundred thousand women belong to the group, which has planted more than forty-five million trees. Green Belters work together to improve their countries. They want future generations to have trees and clean water. They have now moved beyond tree-planting to teach "food security," how to grow foods, such as pigeon peas, pumpkins, and corn. Wangari's idea gave confidence to women who did not realize they had the ability to bring about changes in their communities. They are now empowered to take charge of their lives and the lives of their families.

In 2004, Wangari received word that she would be awarded the Nobel Peace Prize for her contributions to sustainable development, democracy, and peace. She was the first African woman to receive this prize. After winning this notable achievement, Wangari didn't slow down at all. In 2005, she was elected the first president of the African Union's Economic, Social, and Cultural Council and was appointed an ambassador for an initiative to protect the ecosystem of the Congo River Basin. She also won other achievements for her lifetime of work, including an honorary doctorate from Connecticut College in 2006 and the Nichols-Chancellor's Medal from Vanderbilt University in 2011.

Wangari Maathai started the Green Belt Movement with seven saplings in her backyard. She had a vision and made it happen, tree by tree. Some thought she was crazy, some laughed, but she never gave up. Wangari proved that one person can make a difference, that tiny seeds can become forests, and great ideas can become reality. Wangari Maathai passed away in September 2011.

Chapter 9
Aung San Suu Kyi

1945–

What does freedom mean to you? Is it the right to walk down the street without fear? Going to school to learn new and different ideas? Being friends with whomever you choose? Speaking your mind even if it goes against what others think? It's strange how something so hard to describe can be so important. When you live in a country where most people enjoy these and many other freedoms, it is easy to take them for granted. We forget basic human rights are not respected in many parts of the world. Some people even risk their lives for freedom. Aung San Suu Kyi (pronounced awng

In 1989, **Burma** was officially named **Myanmar**. However, the new name is not always recognized by people both in the country and elsewhere in the world, as a way to protest against the military government that made the change.

sahn soo chee) of Burma is one of these people. She is among the world's greatest leaders in the struggle for freedom and democracy.

Burma (Myanmar) is ruled by a brutal military government. The incredibly powerful army uses violence to try to control the thoughts and actions of the people. Children sometimes are taken away from their parents and forced to work as slaves. There are very few schools, so many people never learn to read or write. The average person earns less than a dollar a day. People in Burma can be thrown in jail for criticizing the government, but there are those—like Aung San Suu Kyi—who speak out anyway and refuse to be ruled by fear.

Suu, as she likes to be called, inherited her unbreakable spirit and love for her country from her parents. Her father was General Aung San, commander of the Burma Independence Army. He was a famous champion of justice and democracy who defended Burma against invasions during World War II and worked for its independence, for it had been a British colony. When Suu was two years old, an opposing political

Aung San Suu Kyi (center) with her parents and her two older brothers in 1947. Later that year, her father, Aung San, a Burmese independence leader, was assassinated.

group assassinated her father. She barely had a chance to know him, but grew up knowing of his great deeds and was influenced by his love for Burma. Her mother, Daw Khin Kyi, was head nurse at Rangoon General Hospital (Rangoon is the capital of Burma) and devoted herself to helping sick and injured people.

In 1960, when Suu was fifteen, Daw Khin Kyi became Burma's ambassador to India, and she and Suu moved to New Delhi. Although Suu was away from her homeland, her mother never allowed her to forget her roots. The family's Buddhist faith was also a great comfort. (Buddhism teaches peaceful reflection and does not value material possessions.) Suu was a constant reader who loved learning. While in India, she read about Mahatma Gandhi and his famous nonviolent ways for opposing injustice. He believed violence was wrong and that it was best to solve problems peacefully. Suu liked his ideas because she knew that war hurts everyone.

Suu went to Oxford University in England where she earned degrees in philosophy, politics, and economics in 1967. Living in England was an interesting time. She was different from her classmates, who did not share her religion or country. Suu was not interested in rebelling against authority and always followed school rules—until one day when she decided to experiment.

Many of the English girls in the dormitory would come home from their dates late, after the front gates were locked. The only way in was to climb over a tall wall that surrounded the entire building. Curious about the experience, Suu got a friend to return late with her one night and stay to help boost her over the wall. Her friends found her extreme curiosity amusing but were always willing to support Suu once she got an idea in her head. Another thing she wanted to do was ride a bicycle. Suu had never learned while she was growing up in Rangoon, so friends at Oxford taught her. Although she picked it up quickly, the girls laughed because Suu insisted on riding the bike in her *lungi*, a traditional Burmese sarong. It was awkward, but Suu became an expert at bicycling in a skirt.

After graduation, Suu thought her future would be as an academic, and she moved to New York to get a master's degree. A family friend worked at the United Nations, and Suu took a job there working on the budget. In her spare time, she volunteered at a nearby hospital.

In 1972, she married Michael Aris, a British academic who specialized in Asian literature and history. He was a tutor to the royal family of the kingdom of Bhutan in the Himalayas, and Suu accompanied him there, working as a research officer in the Ministry of Foreign Affairs. Although Suu was almost too busy with her own work to think of getting married, Michael was an intelligent and open-minded person who understood Suu's independent nature and love of Burma. In fact, Suu placed one condition on the marriage: If one day Burma needed her to return, Michael had to be supportive. He agreed.

They moved to England in 1973 and had two sons named Alexander and Kim. It was a busy time for Suu, just the way she liked it. She raised her children, studied at Oxford, and taught courses there about Burma.

Thoughts of her father were never far from Suu's mind. She was fascinated by his accomplishments and began a new project, Aung San's biography. To discover more about his time in Japan, she took a job as visiting scholar at Kyoto University in 1985, and brought Kim along. Michael worked in India and looked after Alexander. The family visited each other every chance they could and were reunited in 1987 when Suu accepted a fellowship in India.

On a quiet evening in 1988, a phone call turned Suu's world upside down. Her mother had suffered a stroke. Suu hung up the phone, packed her suit-cases, and caught a plane to Burma.

Burmese students at class at a school inside the Mae La refugee camp on the Thai border. Many people who have fled to refugee camps have had their land seized and can no longer return home.

The situation in Burma was frightening. Since General Ne Win took over the country in 1958, citizens had lost almost all rights and freedoms. The dictatorship wiped out the consti-tution and replaced government officials with military officers. People were forbidden to disagree with the rulers. Those who did were tortured or killed.

People feared for their lives but could not stand feeling like prisoners. During the early 1980s, people protested all across the country. Many rallies were lead by courageous young students demanding freedom and democracy. On August 8, 1988, there was a countrywide general strike. To beat down the citizens and their desire for basic human rights, the military used violence. Thousands were tortured or shot. However, people did not stop protesting and kept their hopes of freedom alive.

When Suu returned to Burma, she wanted to start a system of libraries in honor of her father, a supporter of literacy and education for all people. But after the August massacres, Suu knew that as Aung San's daughter, she had much more to do.

On August 26, Aung San Suu Kyi gave her first public speech in Burma. Behind her stood a large poster of her father, as if he was there to support her. Several hundred thousand people listened carefully to the daughter of their great, lost leader, as she demanded democracy. With honesty and conviction, she spoke of the importance of peaceful protest and nonviolent resistance. The people knew they were looking at Burma's new voice of freedom.

The democratic movement grew stronger, but the government continued to terrorize its people. The government changed its name to the State Law and Order Restoration Council (SLORC) and arrested hundreds of people without trials. Any political gathering of more than four people was outlawed. It surprised everyone when the

Aung San Suu Kyi speaks at the National League for Democracy party conference in 1996. During the 3-day conference, 250 party members were arrested.

SLORC announced free and fair elections; it seemed they were ready to listen to the people's demands. But the elections were not serious. Because of the laws against political meetings, it was difficult for people to unite and organize. The government assumed no party could win the election.

Suu became the leader of a party called the National League for Democracy (NLD), and risked her life going against the SLORC's laws. Enormous, supportive crowds came to hear her speak. She toured Burma and gave hundreds of speeches. Getting from one place to another was often exhausting. She traveled through the mud and under the burning hot sun, but it had to be done.

There is a famous incident that forms a clear window into the strength of Suu's spirit. On April 5, 1989, she was walking down a road accompanied by other NLD members. A group of stone-faced SLORC soldiers bearing huge rifles stopped them. The head soldier said he would order his men to shoot if anyone took another step forward. Suu motioned for her friends, who were so scared that they could barely breathe, to stay back. She held her head up, stared at the head soldier straight in the eye and kept walking. He ordered his troops to let them pass. Suu is only 5 feet and 4 inches tall (163 cm), and weighs just 106 pounds (48 kg), but she believed in herself. She confronted armed soldiers with only a look—and won.

Suu quickly became an important leader in Burma. In July of 1989, the SLORC put her under house arrest to keep her quiet. It also arrested and tortured important members of the NLD. At first, people were allowed to visit Suu, but the SLORC later refused them entry. Suu could not even receive mail. Completely isolated, except for fifteen guards who watched her day and night, she had to summon all her mental strength to keep from losing faith.

Aung San Suu Kyi makes her way through the crowd of well-wishers after her 2002 release from house arrest. Her freedom was short-lived unfortunately.

The day of the elections came in May 1990. The SLORC was confident that with Suu locked away, people would forget about the NLD. They were wrong. The NLD won the election with 82 percent of the parliamentary seats. The people of Burma had spoken.

But it was not yet time to celebrate. The SLORC ignored the election results, jailed all elected members of the NLD, and kept Suu under house arrest. Suu's spirit could not be broken. Every day she meditated, listened to the news on the radio, played Bach (her favorite composer) on the piano, and read. At times, she became very weak. She often had no money (because she could not work or receive help from her family) and could not afford to eat. Frail and malnourished, Suu lost so much weight that she looked like a skeleton, and her hair fell out. But even starvation did not make her any less determined to see Burma become a free country.

From 1901 to 2003, the Nobel Peace Prize has been awarded to eleven women and eighty men. Out of all the Nobel Prize categories —peace, literature, physics, chemistry, medicine, and economics —more women have won for peace than for any other category.

The story of Burma's fearless would-be leader spread internationally. Amnesty International and the United Nations called for her release. Suu received many awards for her bravery, such as the Sakharov Prize for Freedom of

Thought and the Rafto Prize for Human Rights. She also gained attention with her book called *Freedom from Fear*, a collection of essays that Michael gathered and edited for her. The largest recognition came in 1991, when the Nobel Committee in Norway announced Suu was the winner of the Nobel Peace Prize for her "nonviolent struggle for democracy and human rights." Still a prisoner in her own home, Suu didn't know about the award until she heard it on the radio. The SLORC allowed her to leave the country to receive the prize but on the condition that she could never again return to Burma. Suu refused to play into their hands and stayed home. Alexander and Kim proudly went to Oslo and accepted the award on their mother's behalf.

Suu remained under house arrest until 1995. Although she was officially released, she wasn't free. Suu still was not allowed to see NLD members, her family was not allowed to enter the country, and if she left Burma she could never come back. In 1998, Michael discovered he was dying of cancer. The SLORC hoped Suu would leave Burma to see him, but she could not let them win. Michael asked for special permission to visit Suu one last time. His request was denied and he died one year later.

Aung San Suu Kyi poses for a portrait at NLD headquarters in December of 2010, a month after her release from house arrest.

"It is not power that corrupts but fear. Fear of losing power corrupts those who wield it. Fear of the scourge of power corrupts those who are subject to it."

—AUNG SAN SUU KYI, IN *Freedom from Fear*

Suu continued to spread her message of nonviolence and democracy, but with many difficulties. The government (under the new name of the State Peace and Development Council, or SPDC) watched her very closely and continued to terrorize people. In 2000, Suu was again put under house arrest and released two years later. She also has spent time in Burma's largest jail, Insein Prison, along with many other political prisoners. According to the law, anyone can be arrested, without proof of her or his crime, and with no power to fight back. Several groups and countries called for Suu and other NLD members' freedom, but for a long time the SPDC ignored the demands for justice. Finally, in November of 2010, after being detained for fifteen of the previous twenty-one years, Suu was released from house arrest.

Through everything she went through while under house arrest, Suu remained positive and even made jokes. In one telephone interview, a reporter asked Suu if her phone was tapped. She replied that if it wasn't, she would have to complain to the SLORC because they weren't doing their jobs properly! Born in a country where very few people get to develop their talents, she used every advantage to improve herself and get the truth about Burma out to the world. Suu has faced death many times but never lets fear and anger control her decisions. She lets herself be guided to peaceful protest, and she inspires others to do the same. Some think that only a gun can defeat another gun, but Aung San Suu Kyi believes that education, calm determination, and the truth will set everyone free.

Chapter 10
Roberta Jamieson
1953–

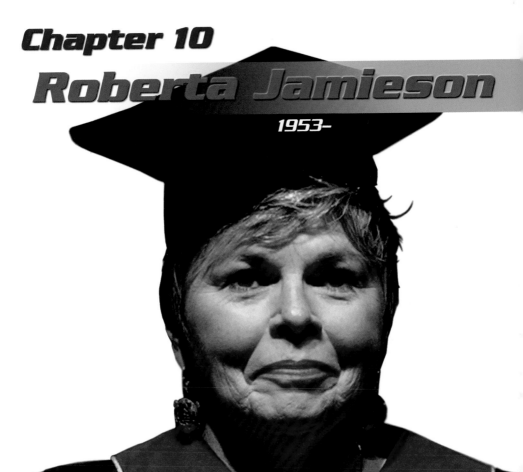

To understand Roberta Jamieson, picture a tree. This tree has a strong, solid trunk, branches reaching to the sky's limitless possibilities, and deep green leaves promising new growth. But what we don't see, the roots, are equally or perhaps even more important. They stretch out underground, like thousands of supporting hands, to keep the tree strong, healthy, and growing. The tree needs its roots to survive and much of Roberta Jamieson's life is based on this idea; look to where you came from to guide you toward where you are going.

Roberta was raised on the Six Nations Reserve of the Grand River Territory, near Brantford, Ontario. From the time she was a young girl, Roberta was very much aware of the ways of her ancestors, the Mohawks. One of the most valuable things she learned was their political tradition of "holding council." When decisions needed to be made, people got together, gave their opinions, and talked about ideas until the best conclusion was reached. Women played an important role in this system as the "conscience of the council," and their opinions and support were taken very seriously.

Roberta loved growing up on the Six Nations Reserve, in a wonderfully close family of seven children and surrounded by those who shared her rich Mohawk culture. Although Roberta's childhood was a happy one, many problems faced and still face Canada's indigenous peoples, some dating back several hundred years.

It used to be said that Europeans "discovered" North America in the 1400s. We now recognize the many indigenous nations who lived here long before the explorers ever imagined that Turtle Island existed. Each group had its own language, political system, and religious and spiritual beliefs, which they passed on through their oral traditions of storytelling and songs.

Turtle Island is the name some First Nations cultures have used for North America because the continent was thought to resemble the shell of a giant turtle surrounded by ocean.

The arrival of the explorers was the beginning of the colonization of North America by the Europeans. Thousands of people came from Europe on boats, drawn by the promise of vast lands, political and religious freedom, adventure, and a new start. Hundreds of thousands more came in chains from Africa as slaves. Not only did Europeans take over First Nations land, but also many indigenous people were forced to change their religions to Christianity, give up their language and culture, and live as the newcomers wanted them to live. Nor did the situation improve significantly over time. As recently as 1927, the Indian Act was passed, which made it illegal for First Nations people to form political groups, speak their own languages, or practice their traditional religions. If they were caught doing any of these things, they could be arrested. Only in the last few decades has this racist, unfair law been changed.

It is important to remember that every First Nations reserve is unique, with its own strengths and weaknesses, just like any community of people. On some reserves, the quality of life is quite good, but other communities face serious problems. One of these problems is poverty; according to the Assembly of First Nations (AFN), the average income of a Native person is about half that of other Canadians. Statistics are similar in the United States. Further troubles are caused by high dropout rates from school, alcoholism, suicide, and health problems such as high rates of tuberculosis and diabetes. In 1996, the AFN calculated that while the infant mortality rate for Canada was 6.1 out of 1,000 children, in First Nations communities

Several different names have been used to identify Canada's indigenous peoples. Early European explorers in North America called them "Indians," apparently thinking they had reached Southeast Asia.

While the name stuck for centuries, today it is generally considered inappropriate, even offensive, in this context.

The terms "First Nations," "Native," and "Aboriginal" all give Canada's indigenous peoples the recognition they have long deserved, as the original inhabitants of the land. They are all used in more or less the same way, though different indigenous communities may prefer one above the others.

"Culture is not something we can take off and put on as if it were a piece of beadwork. We find artifacts in a museum, but if we seek culture, we have to find it in the lives we live."

—ROBERTA JAMIESON

it was 11.6, almost double. Even getting the basic necessities of life can be difficult for many Native people. It is shocking to learn that as late as 1997, the water supplies on 20 percent of reserves were considered unsafe for people to drink. Besides dealing with these serious problems within their communities, First Nations people also face the prejudicial attitudes of those who don't understand their situation and history.

Roberta Jamieson knew all about the hardships First Nations people have faced both now and throughout history. Early on, she knew she would choose a career that would involve helping others. Not one to stand back and accept everything she heard as true and unchangeable, even as a child Roberta was full of questions. Her father, who had an important influence on her childhood, always encouraged his daughter to be curious and ambitious. Roberta decided to become a doctor because not only would it be a challenging, useful job, it would also make her father proud, for he had the same dream when he was a boy.

Determined to make her own positive contribution to the world and to help make life better for First Nations people, Roberta enrolled in medical school at Montreal's McGill University in 1970. This was an impressive achievement because at the time few Native people graduated from high school, let alone went to college. Most young students preferred to live as close to campus as possible, but Roberta insisted on living just outside the city on the Kahnawake Reserve because she did not want to lose sight of her roots.

Being in a different province, far away from family, is never easy; living among people who understood her history and culture made her less homesick.

It was during this time that Roberta discovered that her true passion was not medicine but politics and social justice. The government of Quebec had plans to build a hydroelectric dam on territory belonging to the Cree of James Bay. It did not, however, plan to get permission from the land's rightful owners or offer to pay for any damage to the land or fishing areas. Roberta was furious at the way the government ignored the rights of First Nations people. How could she join the fight to help them get the justice they deserved?

In 1974, when she was only twenty-one years old, Roberta debated the Cree land claims issue with Jean Chrétien, then the Minister of Indian Affairs (and later Canada's Prime Minister). While many might be afraid of an opponent who not only held a position of power but also was much older, Roberta refused to be frightened. She gave a speech that was both passionate and well argued, and the listeners agreed that Chrétien was definitely upstaged. This experience demonstrated to Roberta the truth in Mohawk traditions; an intelligent, informed argument has more power than resorting to anger.

The James Bay Cree incident made Roberta decide to leave medical school and enroll in law school at the University of Western Ontario in London. While there, she helped start the Native Law Students Association. She finished her degree in 1976, the first Native woman in Canada to graduate from law school. Although Roberta was very proud of this achievement, she couldn't help but wonder why it took so long for a Native woman in Canada to reach such a goal. Obviously, there was a lot of work to be

> "Mohawk people have always placed a lot of importance on diplomacy. We've placed a lot of influence on process, on reaching a consensus, knowing that if you spend the time to come to a genuine consensus it will be long-lasting."
>
> —Roberta Jamieson

done. Ready to continue her dream of protecting the rights of First Nations people, Roberta worked for important Native groups over the next ten years. Fresh out of school, she joined the federal Canadian Indian Rights Commission, and next the Indian Rights Commission of Ontario; she became its first female president in 1985. Because of her reputation as a dedicated and fair leader within the First Nations community, she was asked to join a committee on Native self-government. It was a unique position to be in because Roberta was the first and only person on the committee who was not a member of Parliament. Her work involved a lot of patience and hard work, but Roberta was always looking to challenge herself and the world around her.

Someone who helps two opposing sides reach an agreement is called a mediator, and it was clear from the work Roberta had done negotiating for the rights of First Nations people that she had found her calling. She continued to use the tradition of holding council, believing decisions should be reached by discussion and consultation in a cool-headed manner, rather than through angry confrontation. This is Roberta's signature style, and one of the reasons she is such a trusted negotiator.

Roberta took on a new challenge in 1989 that allowed her to use and share her mediation skills with the people of Ontario; she became the provincial ombudsman. She was the perfect person for this position because of her fairness and experience in resolving conflict. As ombudsman, her job was first to explore complaints or problems citizens might have when dealing with the province's government organizations, then to suggest the best possible solution. Roberta and her colleagues helped resolve problems with many issues, such as family support payments, access to healthcare, treatment of prisoners, and safety at work. Most of us would find dealing with complaints all day very frustrating (in her ten years as ombudsman, her office handled over

Members of the Huu-ay-aht First Nation burn a copy of Canada's Indian Act.

three hundred thousand complaints), but Roberta's gift for understanding and explaining both sides of an argument assisted her search for justice for people who felt they were being treated unfairly. She knew she was helping others by showing the power of negotiation.

Although as ombudsman, Roberta still had contact with First Nations communities, she felt it was time to use what she had learned to work with those closest to her heart. Her years of leadership experience, knowledge of how the government works, and desire to reach fair solutions would be helpful to the First Nations, and in 2001, Roberta made history yet again. She was elected the first woman chief of the Six Nations of the Grand River Territory, the same territory where she grew up and has lived most of her life. With approximately twenty-one thousand members, it is the largest First Nations community in Canada.

In July 2003, Roberta ran for the leadership of the Assembly of First Nations (AFN), a group representing approximately 630 Native groups across Canada. Although she was not elected, it was a very close race, and Roberta finished in second place. She faced tough competition; the other two candidates were Phil Fontaine (the winner) and Matthew Coon Come, both longtime leaders within Canada's Native communities. True to her character, Roberta accepted the defeat with a radiant smile and acknowledged the fact that the voters' decision, although not the one she wanted, was reached by fair election and was to be respected.

Although Roberta's work has kept her very busy, family has always been as important to her as when she was a girl. She still lives on the Six Nations Reserve with her husband, Tom Hill, who shares Roberta's passion for promoting the culture of indigenous people. Tom is known worldwide as an expert on First Nations' history and works with museums in Canada and the United States. The couple has a daughter, Jessica. When she was a little girl she showed signs of intelligence and curiosity, just like her mother.

Roberta Jamieson will always devote herself to issues that are important to Native people. In particular, she plans to keep up her fight against the passing of the First Nations Governance Act, also called Bill C-7. This law is supposed to give First Nations people the power to make decisions and handle affairs in their own communities. However, Roberta and many others believe that it should be up to Native people to develop their own systems of governance, systems that show their cultural values, rather than forcing the laws and systems of another, non-Native, culture on them.

An inspirational figure to First Nations people, women, and leaders everywhere, Roberta has received many awards during her career. For her dedication to First Nations' causes, she received an Outstanding Contribution Award from the National Indian Brotherhood, a National Aboriginal Achievement Award, and the Indigenous Peoples Council Award. Her work in promoting equality for all people in society was recognized with the Harmony Award and the Deo Kernahan Memorial Award by the Urban Alliance on Race Relations in Toronto. In 1994, she was made a member of the Order of Canada and has also been given honorary degrees from eight Canadian universities and the Law Society of Upper Canada.

Roberta Jamieson is "a woman of firsts." But while she knows she has been the first—as a First Nations person and as a woman—to accomplish many things, it is not praise or awards that keep her going. She feels she is simply putting her talents to good use, doing what she was meant to do. There is no denying that First Nations people have many difficulties to surmount; it is why Roberta's work is so important. She is fueled by the idea of making Canada a better place, a country that respects the people whose land and resources made the country what it is today. For this reason, Roberta was appointed the chief executive officer of the National Aboriginal Achievement Foundation (NAAF). This organization is proudly devoted to celebrating the achievements of Canada's Aboriginal Peoples. Roberta continues to hold this post to this day. Despite everything that seemed to be against her, from the difficulties of her ancestors to the prejudices of the present, Roberta never let anything get in the way of her goals. Her life is a great example that we should never be afraid to try and never get discouraged by the idea that if something has not been done before, it cannot be done at all.

Roberta Jamieson has had an amazing career as a leader who proved that by getting together, talking about our problems and giving everyone a voice, great things can be achieved. She found her path by remembering the cultural values of her Mohawk heritage, and that her roots are what help to make her a strong woman. Surely, Roberta Jamieson will continue to flourish and grow.

Chapter 11
Shirin Ebadi
1947–

In many countries, young girls and boys are taught that they can be whatever they want when they grow up. However, in some parts of the world, young girls are taught that many of the world's opportunities are closed to them. Shirin Ebadi grew up in one of these places, but refused to believe that she couldn't do whatever she set her mind to. She is at once a feminist, a tireless advocate for human rights, and a champion for the voices of unheard women and children. She has served as both a judge and a lawyer in a country where being either is nearly impossible for a woman.

Shirin was born in the city of Hamedan in northwestern Iran on June 21, 1947. Her parents were both academics and followers of the religion of Islam. Her father, Mohammad Ali Ebad, was the minister of Hamedan's Registry Office. He also worked as a professor of law. Her mother was also an academic and devoted her life to the education and upbringing of Shirin and her two sisters and brother. Her mother had a strong impact on Shirin's life. She has said that she is the person she is today because of her mother's love.

When Shirin was only a year old, her family moved to Tehran, the capital city of Iran. She had a very happy childhood. Her parents treated her and all her sisters and brother equally. Later, Shirin would learn this treatment was unusual. In Iran, boys and girls are often treated differently by their parents. Boys are usually given more attention by their fathers. They are also allowed more freedom than girls, who are expected to be quiet and obedient.

Shirin began her education at a primary school in Tehran called Firuzkuhi primary school and went on to Anoshiravn Dadgar and Reza Shah Kabir secondary schools for her higher education. When she was older, she went to Tehran University to study law. She had decided she wanted to be a judge. Three and a half years later, in 1965, she graduated from the university with a degree in law. Shirin wasn't one to let the earth cool under her feet for long. Right after graduating, she took the entrance exam for the Department of Justice.

After passing the exam, she found a six-month apprenticeship in adjudication. Adjudication is the study of being a judge. Shirin worked under the guidance of another judge to learn how to use the evidence in a case to make sound and reasonable decisions. In March of 1969, after her apprenticeship was completed, Shirin officially began to work as a judge.

But Shirin didn't stop her education just because she had a job to keep her busy. She continued to study while working. In 1971, she received a doctorate with honors in private law from Tehran University. Private law is a special branch of legal studies that deals with deciding cases between two people or even between large groups of people.

What is remarkable about Shirin's long course of studies and eventual rise to serving as a judge is where Shirin lived. In Iran, women did not serve as judges. In fact, Shirin was the

Human rights activist Shirin Ebadi shows her Nobel Prize diploma during the 2003 Nobel Peace Prize ceremony in Oslo.

first woman in the history of Iranian justice to serve as a judge. That's quite an accomplishment! She also served many different positions in the Department of Justice. In 1975, she became the president of a bench of the City Court of Tehran. This position made her a chief justice. She was also the first woman in Iran to ever serve as a chief justice.

However, in February of 1979, everything changed in Iran. An Islamic Revolution moved through the country. Iran's monarchy was overthrown, and a new republic was formed under the rule of Ayatollah Ruhollah Khomeini. A new government and constitution were instated based on the religion of Islam. This made the country a much more difficult place for the women who lived there. Under Islamic Law, women must cover themselves when they go outside and must dress and wear their hair a certain way so that it cannot be seen. Another new rule in the country based on Islamic Law was that women could no longer be judges. Shirin and all the other female judges were dismissed from their posts and made to do clerical work for the judges who were men. In Shirin's case, they made her a clerk for the very court she had once presided over.

Shirin protested the law. She was herself a Muslim woman. However, she did not agree with religious laws being forced on a country or a religion being used as an excuse to take the rights of women away. As a result of her protests, the government promoted Shirin and many other female judges to the position of "experts" in the Justice Department. However, they were still not allowed to return to their former posts as judges.

Shirin could not tolerate being treated like a second-class citizen because she was a woman, so she put in a request to retire early. Her request was accepted. After that, she decided she would become a lawyer and practice law from the other side of the bench. However, in order to become a lawyer, she had to put in an application to the Bar Association. Unfortunately, the Bar Association had been shut down after the Revolution in 1979. Her application instead was looked at by the same government-run Justice Department that had refused to allow her to continue being a judge. Not surprisingly, her application was turned down. For many years, Shirin kept mostly to her house because she was no longer allowed to work in the field she loved.

While she was unemployed against her will, Shirin used her time to write a number of books and articles. She knew that an injustice had been done against her and the women of Iran; however, she didn't focus on just this, but rather all the injustices she saw committed in the world around her. In 1987, she wrote a book on the rights of children and how they were treated in Iran. This book was later translated into English and published by the United Nations Children's Fund (known as UNICEF). In 1989, she wrote a book about the rights of workers and child labor. In 1993, she wrote a book called *The Rights of Refugees*. In this book, Shirin wrote about the legal aspects of being a refugee in Iran. She discussed controversial issues like the right to an education and to personal property, and looked at both the laws of her country as well as international refugee laws.

Throughout the years, Shirin did not give up on her dream and continued to apply to be a lawyer. In 1992, Shirin was finally able to obtain a lawyer's license. She set up her own practice where clients could hire her to take on cases. First and foremost, she was still concerned with the rights of women and children, and overall the basic rights of all humans. She came to specialize in cases involving human rights violations.

In 1999, Shirin took on a case involving the murders of a man named Dariush Forouhar and his wife Parvaneh Eskandari Forouhar. Dariush Forouhar was himself a human rights activist who had been speaking out against the government of Iran. When he and his wife were found murdered in their home, many people suspected the murders were politically motivated. Shirin was able to use evidence to connect the murders back to the Iranian Ministry of Intelligence. The head of this organization, Saeed Emami, took his own life before he could be formally charged with the murders of the Forouhars.

In addition to her legal work, Shirin continues to be

Shirin Ebadi participates in a round table discussion in 2004 with several other great leaders and advocates for peace, including the Dalai Lama and Desmond Tutu.

an outspoken advocate for the rights of all people. In 1995, she co-founded the Association for the Support of Children's Rights and served as its president until 2000. She was also instrumental in helping to write and push for a law prohibiting all violence against children in Iran. The law was passed in the summer of 2002. In 2001, she also helped found the Human Rights Defense Centre (HRDC), and served as its president for several years.

In 2003, Shirin was awarded the Nobel Peace Prize for her commitment to human rights, and especially for her struggles to help women and children. She was the first Iranian person to win this prize. She was also the first Muslim woman to do so.

Shirin continues to fight against injustice even as the country of Iran becomes more turbulent. The government of Iran continues to be hostile toward Shirin's efforts. In 2009, while Shirin was traveling abroad giving lectures and attending conferences around the world, the government of Iran seized her Nobel Prize medal and certificate from a safe deposit box in Tehran. She also receives threats on her life for her work.

It would be easy for Shirin to give up and to allow fear to keep her from working tirelessly as an advocate for women, children, and the rights of humans. However, Shirin refuses to let fear or intimidation keep her from her missions. When asked how she manages to deal with the pressure to stop her work, Shirin says: "How can you defy fear? Fear is a human instinct, just like hunger. Whether you like it or not, you become hungry. Similarly with fear. But I have learned to train myself to live with this fear. Human rights is a universal standard. It is a component of every religion and every civilization." And Shirin will continue to not let fear stop her, as she continues to voice her opinion in a land where women's voices are so often kept from being heard.

Glossary

activist A person who uses direct action to bring about change for an important cause.

boycott A refusal, usually by a group of people, to have dealings with a person, business, or organization to express disapproval or to force acceptance of certain conditions.

consensus A general agreement among a group of people.

democracy A government in which power is placed in the hands of the people, through a system of representation involving periodically held elections.

diptheria A bacterial infection, usually involving the nose and throat, and can result in airway blockage, skin lesions, and severe cough.

feminist A person who believes in equal rights between women and men.

heritage Something inherited from the past, whether it be physical or cultural attributes.

hydroelectric The production of electricity by water power.

indigenous Living or growing naturally in a particular region.

kibbutz A communal farm or settlement in Israel.

kohl A black or dark cosmetic used around the eyes by women, particularly in the Middle East and Egypt.

mediation The act of intervening between two conflicting parties to promote reconciliation, settlement, or compromise.

pamphlet An unbound publication.

patriarchal Of or relating to men as a group.

pharaoh The highest ranking ruler of ancient Egypt.

prejudice A preconceived judgment or opinion, often about a race, culture, sex, or sexual orientation.

sapling A young tree.

segregation The separation or isolation of a race, class, or ethnic group.

suffrage The political right to vote.

suffragist A person, man or woman, who supports equal voting rights.

For More Information

Global Fund for Women
222 Sutter Street, Suite 500
San Francisco, CA 94108
(415) 248-4800
Web site: http://www.globalfundforwomen.org
This organization plays a leading role in advancing women's
    rights by making grants that support and strengthen
    women's groups around the world.

Green Belt Movement (U.S. Office)
1666 K Street NW, Suite 440
Washington, DC 20006
(202) 457-8080
Web site: http://greenbeltmovement.org
Founded by Wangari Maathai, this organization promotes
    human rights, good governance, and peaceful demo-
    cratic change through protection of the environment.

International Campaign to Ban Landmines
9 Rue de Cornavin
CH-1201 Geneva
Switzerland
Web site: http://www.icbl.org
This is a Nobel Peace Prize–winning global network in over
    ninety countries that works for a world free of antiper-
    sonnel landmines, where landmine survivors can lead
    fulfilling lives.

National Organization for Women
1100 H Street NW, 3rd Floor

Washington, DC 20005

(202) 628-8669

Web site: http://www.now.org

This is the largest organization of feminist activists in the United States.

Rosa & Raymond Parks Institute for Self Development

535 Griswold Street, Suite 111-513

Detroit, MI 48226

(313) 965-0606

Web site: http://www.rosaparks.org

This organization founded by Rosa Parks and Elaine Eason Steele helps motivate youth to reach their highest potential.

Women's Rights National Historical Park

136 Fall Street

Seneca Falls, NY 13148

(315) 568-0024

Web site: http://www.nps.gov/wori/index.htm

This is the historical park and location of the first Women's Rights Convention, organized by Elizabeth Cady Stanton and four other women.

Web Sites

Due to the changing nature of Internet links, Rosen Publishing has developed an online list of Web sites related to the subject of this book. This site is updated regularly. Please use this link to access the list:

http://www.rosenlinks.com/gwoa/lead

For Further Reading

Adler, David A. *Our Golda: The Story of Golda Meir.* New York, NY: Viking, 1984.

Amdur, Richard. *Golda Meir: A Leader in Peace and War.* New York, NY: Fawcett Columbine, 1990.

Ancient Egypt: Discovering Its Splendors. Washington, D.C.: National Geographic Society, 1978.

Andronik, Catherine M. *Hatshepsut: His Majesty, Herself.* New York, NY: Antheneum Books for Young Readers, 2001.

Aung San Suu Kyi. *Letters from Burma.* New York, NY: Penguin, 2010.

Bearden, Jim, and Linda Jean Butler. *Shadd: The Life and Times of Mary Shadd Cary.* Toronto, Canada: New Canada Publications, 1997.

Bertrand, Real. *Therese Casgrain.* Montreal, Canada: Lidec, Inc., 1981.

Brinkley, Douglas. *Rosa Parks: A Life.* New York, NY: Penguin, 2005.

Browne, Ray B., ed. *Contemporary Heroes and Heroines.* Detroit, MI: Gale Research, 1990.

Burkett, Elinor. *Golda.* New York, NY: Harper, 2008.

Casgrain, Therese F. *A Woman in a Man's World.* Toronto, Canada: McClelland & Stewart, 1972.

Celsi, Teresa. *Rosa Parks and the Montgomery Bus Boycott.* Brookfield, CT: The Millbrook Press, 1991.

Colman, Penny. *Elizabeth Cady Stanton and Susan B. Anthony: A Friendship That Changed the World.* New York, NY: Henry Holt, 2011.

Cullen-Du-Pont, Kathryn. *Elizabeth Cady Stanton and Women's Liberty.* New York: Facts on File, 1992.

Cuomo, Kerry Kennedy. *Speak Truth to Power*. New York, NY: Crown, 2002.

Davidson, True. *The Golden Strings*. Toronto, Canada: Griffin House, 1973.

Dell, Pamela. *Hatshepsut: Egypt's First Female Pharaoh*. Mankato, MN: Compass Point, 2008.

Ebadi, Shirin. *The Golden Cage: Three Brothers, Three Choices, One Destiny*. Carlsbad, CA: Kales Press, 2011.

Ebadi, Shirin. *Iran Awakening: One Woman's Journey to Reclaim Her Life and Country*. New York, NY: Random House, 2007.

Feinberg, Leslie. *Transgender Warriors: Making History for Joan of Arc to RuPaul*. Boston, MA: Beacon, 1996.

"Fontaine Wins AFN Leadership on Second Ballot." *The Toronto Star*, online edition, July 16, 2003.

Friese, Kai. *Rosa Parks: The Movement Organizes*. Englewood Cliffs, NJ: Silver Burdett Press, 1990.

Fritz, Jean. *You Want Women to Vote, Lizzie Stanton?* New York, NY: G.P. Putman's Sons, 1995.

Galford, Ellen. *World History Biographies: Hatshepsut: The Princess Who Became King*. Des Moines, IA: National Geographic, 2007.

Genovese, Michael A., ed. *Women as National Leaders*. Newbury Park, CA: Sage Publications, 1993.

Gizberg, Lori D. *Elizabeth Cady Stanton: An American Life*. New York, NY: Hill and Wang, 2010.

Greenblatt, Miriam. *Hatshepsut and Ancient Egypt*. New York, NY: Benchmark Books, 2000.

Hill, Daniel G. *The Freedom-Seekers: Blacks in Early Canada*. Toronto, Canada: The Book Society of Canada Limited, 1981.

"Interview with Roberta Jamieson, Six Nations Elected Chief, Regarding the Impacts of Canada's Proposed First Nations Governance Act," *Indian Country*, July 15, 2002.

James, Donna. *Emily Murphy*. Toronto, Canada: Fitzhenry and Whiteside, 1977.

Klein, Edward. "The Lady Triumphs," *Vanity Fair*. October 1995, 120–144.

Lappe, Frances Moore and Anna Lappe. *Hope's Edge: The Next Diet for a Small Planet*. New York, NY: Putnam, 2002.

Maathai, Wangari. *The Challenge for Africa*. New York, NY: Anchor, 2010.

Maathai, Wangari. *Unbowed: A Memoir*. New York, NY: Anchor, 2007.

Mander, Christine. *Emily Murphy: Rebel*. Toronto, Canada: Simon and Pierre, 1995.

Meir, Golda. *My Life*. London, England: Weidenfeld and Nicolson, 1975.

Parks, Rosa and Jim Haskins. *Rosa Parks: My Story*. New York, NY: Puffin, 1992.

Price-Groff, Claire. *Twentieth-Century Women Political Leaders*. New York, NY: Facts on File, 1998.

Quirke, Stephen and Jeffrey Spencer. *The British Museum Book of Ancient Egypt*. New York, NY: Thames and Hudson, 1992.

Rhodes, Jane. *Mary Ann Shadd Cary: The Black Press and Protest in the Nineteenth Century*. Bloomington: Indiana University Press, 1998.

Ringgold, Faith. *If a Bus Could Talk: The Story of Rosa Parks*. New York, NY: Simon & Schuster for Young Readers, 1999.

Sadlier, Rosemary. *Mary Ann Shadd: Publisher, Editor, Teacher, Lawyer, Suffragette*. Toronto, Canada: Umbrella Press, 1995.

Sanders, Byrne Hope. *Famous Women: Carr, Hind, Gullen, Murphy*. Toronto, Canada: Clarke, Irwin, 1958.

Sears, Priscilla. "You Strike the Woman..." *Making It Happen* (Spring 1991), p. 55.

Stetson Clarke, Mary. *Bloomers and Ballots: Elizabeth Cady Stanton and Women's Rights.* New York, NY: Viking, 1972.

Stewart, Whitney. *Aung San Suu Kyi: Fearless Voice of Burma.* Minneapolis, MN: Lerner, 1997.

Wallace, Aubrey. *Eco-Heroes: Twelve Tales of Environmental Victory.* San Francisco, CA: Mercury House, 1993.

Ward, Geoffrey C., and Ken Burns. *Not for Ourselves Alone: The Story of Elizabeth Cady Stanton and Susan B. Anthony.* New York, NY: Knopf, 1999.

Wheeler, Jill C. *Rosa Parks.* Edina, MN: ABDO, 2003.

Wintle, Justin. *Perfect Hostage: A Life of Aunt San Suu Kyi, Burma's Prisoner of Conscience.* New York, NY: Skyhorse, 2008.

Index

About the Author

Heather Ball is a professional writer and editor and a graduate of the Humber School for Writers. She has reviewed books for *Broken Pencil* magazine, and in 2003, she was named Centennial College's first ever Writer of the Year. She lives and works in Toronto.

Photo Credits

Cover (top), p. 65 Charley Gallay/Getty Images; cover (bottom) Pornchai Kittiwongsakul/AFP/Getty Images; p. 7 Kenneth Garrett/National Geographic Image Collection/ Getty Images; pp. 8, 45, 53 Shutterstock.com; p. 11 Kean Collection/Archive Photos/Getty Images; p. 13 iStockphoto/ Thinkstock; pp. 15, 18, 21 © Everett Collection/SuperStock; p. 19 National Park Service; p. 23 Library and Archives Canada/C-029977; p. 27 A Plea for Emigration, or, Notes of Canada West, 1852. Courtesy of Toronto Public Library; p. 28 Provincial Freeman, November 18, 1854. Courtesy of Toronto Public Library; p. 31 City of Edmonton Archives EA-10-1983; p. 35 City of Edmonton Archives EA-10-1995; p. 36 City of Edmonton Archives EA-596-303 Wetherill; p. 39 Yousuf Karsh/Library and Archives Canada/PA-178196; p. 43 Status of Women Canada/Library and Archives Canada/ e002415955; p. 47 Gemma Levine/Premium Archive/Getty Images; pp. 50, 55, 60, 71, 76, 80, 91 © AP Images; p. 52 Hulton Archive/Getty Images; p. 58 Buyenlarge/Archive Photos/Getty Images; p. 59 Stan Wayman/Time & Life Pictures/Getty Images; pp. 69, 70 Tony Karumba/AFP/ Getty Images; p. 72 Simon Maina/AFP/Getty Images; pp. 75, 97 AFP/Getty Images; p. 79 Nicolas Asfouri/AFP/Getty Images; p. 82 Stephen Shaver/AFP/Getty Images; p. 83 Drn/Getty Images; p. 85 Ken Faught/Toronto Star/ZUMA Press/Newscom; p. 95 Dan Tuffs/Getty Images; p. 99 Don MacKinnon/Getty Images; interior graphic (globe) © www. istockphoto.com/Selahattin Bayram.